American Med

Physicians dedicated to th

MW00676638

Managing
the Medical Practice
Second Edition

Crystal S. Reeves
The Coker Group

Practice Success Series

Managing the Medical Practice
Second Edition

Internet address: www.ama-assn.org

This book is for informational purposes only. It is not intended to constitute legal or financial advice. If legal, financial, or other professional advice is required, the services of a competent professional should be sought.

Additional copies of this book may be ordered by calling 800-621-8335.
Secure online orders can be taken at www.ama-assn.org/catalog.
Mention product number OP701202

ISBN 1-57947-292-3

Library of Congress Cataloging-in-Publication Data

Reeves, Crystal S.
    Managing the medical practice /Crystal S. Reeves ; the Coker Group.--2nd ed.
        p. ; cm. -- (Practice success! series)
    Rev. ed. of: Managing the medical practice / American Medical Association. c1996.
    Includes bibliographical references and index.
    ISBN 1-57947-292-3
    1. Medicine--Practice--United States--Management--Handbooks, manuals, etc. 2. Medical offices--United States--Management--Handbooks, manuals, etc. I. Coker Group. II. Title. III. Series.
    [DNLM: 1. Practice Management, Medical--organization & administration--Handbooks. W 49 R332m 2002]
    R728.R435 2002
    610'.68--dc21

2002010739

BQ13:02-P-042:10/02

The Coker Group, a leader in health care consulting, helps providers attain improved financial and operational results through sound business principles. The consulting team members are proficient, trustworthy professionals with experience and strengths in various areas. The well-rounded staff includes seasoned individuals in finance, administration, management, operations, compliance, personnel management, and information systems.

The Coker Group's nationwide client base includes major health systems, hospitals, physician groups, and solo practitioners in a full spectrum of engagements. The Coker Group has gained a reputation since 1987 for thorough, efficient, and cost-conscious work to benefit its clients financially and operationally. The firm has a towering profile with recognized and respected health care professionals throughout the industry. Coker's exceptional consulting team has health care, technical, financial, and business knowledge and offers comprehensive programs, services, and training to yield long-term solutions and turnarounds. Coker staff members are devoted to delivering reliable answers and dependable options so that decision-makers can make categorical decisions. Coker consultants enable providers to concentrate on patient care.

Service Areas

- Practice management, billing and collection reviews, chart audits
- Procedural coding analysis
- Information systems review, including EMR
- Physician employment and compensation review
- Physician network development
- Practice appraisals
- Strategic planning/business planning
- Disengagements of practices and network unwinds
- Practice operational assessments
- Contract negotiations
- Hospital services, medical staff development
- Practice start-ups
- Buy/sell and equity analysis
- Sale/acquisition negotiations
- Group formation and dissolution
- Educational programs, workshops, and training
- Compliance plans
- HIPAA assessments and compliance
- MSA development

- Financial analysis
- Mediation and expert witnessing
- Policies and procedures manuals

For more information, contact:

The Coker Group
11660 Alpharetta Hwy / Suite 710 / Roswell, GA 30076 /
800.345.5829 www.cokergroup.com

Crystal S. Reeves holds the position of principal of The Coker Group, a national health care services firm specializing in physician development programs and other associated services. In this position, she is responsible for managing the delivery of services to physicians, both through client hospitals and to individual practices.

With more than 26 years experience in health care and medical practice management, both in primary care and multispecialty practices, Ms Reeves is a recognized leader in medical practice management in areas pertaining to implementing and refining billing and collection services, improving operations, and physician and staff education. Ms. Reeves is a sought-after speaker and consultant presenting seminars nationwide on coding and reimbursement, documentation guidelines, front desk operations, and customer service. She is a regular faculty member at MGMA Annual Conferences and Georgia MGMA Conferences. She has also been a speaker at United Communication Group's Physician Coding Summit on billing for nonphysician practitioners.

Ms Reeves has authored several books, including the first and second editions of a guidebook for the Renal Physicians Association titled *The Renal Physicians Guide to Nephrology Practice* ©1999 and ©2001 (Coker Consulting, LLC and Renal Physicians Association); *IPA Management: Legal and Compliance Guidelines* ©1999 (McGraw-Hill); *Assessing and Improving Staffing and Organization* ©2000 (American Medical Association); and *Compliance for Physician Practices: A 7-Step Plan* ©2001 (Management Concepts).

Ms Reeves is certified by the American Academy of Professional Coders and is a member of the American College of Medical Practice Executives. Additionally, she serves on the Editorial Board for *Part B Insider*, a publication of St Anthony Publishing.

Three trends in health care will shape the way medical practices are managed in the twenty-first century. The trends are:

1. Consumers will be king
2. Technology will change expectations
3. Partnerships will be important

Managing the Medical Practice is about successfully functioning as a business enterprise, while serving patients as consumers of health care—consumers with demands and high expectations. It is also about working with technology to enhance efficiency and with ultimate effectiveness to create and sustain a viable work environment. And *Managing the Medical Practice* is about partnering with other providers and health care entities, not so much as business associates, but as professional entities that join together to provide the highest level of patient care imaginable.

The purpose of this book is to present and answer fundamental questions of management and daily operations that will assist practices in their pursuit of the highest level of efficiency and ingenuity to meet today's and tomorrow's challenges. The information in this book calls for some changes to commonly accepted routines that have been established in many physician practices throughout the past decades. It addresses old traditions and offers new ideas for re-engineering operations.

Managing the Medical Practice is about:

■ Reinventing the organization by discarding long-held beliefs about how to create and deliver products and services

■ Attempting to redesign the total work process by compiling a series of inputs and tasks to enhance value

■ Assessing how the practice delivers health care services and why it does it that way

■ Rethinking the total delivery process and redesigning the appropriate support systems

■ Succeeding when physicians and administrators realize and accept that simply to enhance, modify, or superficially improve work tasks will not support the future practice delivery system

While reviewing this book, take a fresh look at every function in the practice and consider the way it is done and who does it. Be willing to discard or reassign tasks when another solution is more appropriate. Get processes, policies, and procedures in place and cultivate them—but never let up on looking introspectively for better ways to accomplish tasks. This book is filled with handy tools for assessment and completion of a myriad of day-to-day events and duties in the medical practice.

CONTENTS

x   Contents

4 Training and Education   53

5 Managing Staff/Team Building   59

6 Employment Law   73

chapter 1

The Role of Manager

Office manager, practice manager, practice administrator—whatever the title the practice bestows upon this position of leadership for the organization, the person in the role acts as the physician's agent in employee supervision, patient relations, collection of fees, and the control of practice expenses. For that reason, it is vitally important to carefully select an experienced, knowledgeable, and intelligent person for the role of manager.

Sometimes, it is difficult for practices to determine exactly what kind and how much expertise they need for their practice management position. Sometimes, they are reluctant to hand over managerial responsibilities to anyone, preferring to oversee the management issues themselves. Sometimes, they hire a manager by credentials alone, such as BA, MBA, or RN, without asking themselves, "Does this person have the expertise to manage this office now and to help us get where we want to go?" If the wrong person is in the job, physicians may get the feeling that something has gone awry with the system, yet they are not able to identify the point at which "it just isn't working."

Common errors in selecting a manager include hiring a manager for a small practice of one or two physicians, and then failing to evaluate the effectiveness of the manager as the organization grows. Other physicians believe that because their nurse is so effective at managing people, she can assume the role of practice manager—while maintaining her current role as nurse. Still others make the mistake of focusing only on the salary expectations of the potential applicants or being swayed by an impressive list of initials after the applicant's name.

In considering the management of many individuals and their livelihood, none of the aforementioned manager-selection methods are appropriate. In fact, studies have shown that when a practice manager fails, it is usually due to one of two things: Either the wrong person was hired for the role, or once the right person was hired, that individual's ability to do their job was impeded.

Therefore, the first step to developing a successful practice is to determine the management needs of the practice and to find the person that can meet those needs.

DETERMINING THE NEEDS OF THE PRACTICE

Terms used for the key management position of a practice are often confusing and can include titles such as office manager, practice manager, and practice administrator. The role of this leader, however, varies greatly. The general differences between these management titles are outlined in Table 1-1.

TABLE 1-1

Evaluating Managerial Needs

	Office Manager	Practice Manager	Practice Administrator
Level of Authority	An office manager rarely initiates; he/she responds to physician directives	A practice manager is an initiator of projects and ideas generated by him/her and the physician team. Physicians participate in the process	A practice administrator is a business leader who directs a team of capable managers or team leaders. Physicians set policies, but do little directing
Number of Full-Time Physicians	1– Approximately 3	Approximately 3 – 8	Approximately 8+
Number of Physician Extenders	0	Often 1 or more	Often 2 or more
Types of Business Units	Typically, office practice only	Office practice; maybe ancillaries, such as X-ray, audiology, rehab, physical therapy; product sales; maybe surgery suite	Office practice; maybe ancillaries, such as X-ray, audiology, rehab, physical therapy; product sales; maybe surgery suite; maybe drug studies or research
Number of Full-Time Staff	Approximately 3 – 10	Approximately 10+	Approximately 20+
Annual Practice Revenue	Up to $1 million	Approximately $1 million to $6 million	Over $6 million
Number of Practice Sites	1 primary site	1 primary site, 1–2 satellites	1 primary site; multiple satellites
Maturity of Managed Care Market	Typically, less than 20%; often located in rural or remote setting where fee-for-service reimbursement still dominates; not many contracts signed yet; physicians and staff still in "Golden Age of Medicine" mindset	Typically, more than 20%; business coalitions forming; some primary care physicians are capitated; physicians looking for ways to increase market share and gain exclusivity with plans	Typically, more than 20%; some specialists are capitated; business coalitions hold power; employer-direct contracts prevalent; case rates common; large primary care and multi-specialty groups—or physician practice management companies—steer significant patient flow
Degree of Market Integration	Solos and small groups prevail; probably an IPA and/or PHO in place	Physicians groups are growing in size; hospitals and physicians work together; primary care physicians are owned by hospitals or national management companies; several IPAs and possibly an MSO have been developed	Multi-specialty groups in place; health "system" quite evolved; primary care physicians are owned; information systems are shared among hospitals; physicians
Number of Capitated Contracts	0 or sometimes 1	2, 3, or 4	

Source: Zupko, K. Why MD's are disappointed with practice administrators and managers. *The Journal of Medical Practice Management*; 15(5)
©2000 Greenbranch Publishing LLC, 800-933-3711. Used with permission.

How much "management" does the practice need? That answer depends on many things. Among the considerations are:

- The organizational structure of the practice
- The physicians' role in leadership
- The number of physicians and mid-level providers
- Practice revenues and budget
- Whether the practice is in a growth mode or developed and stable
- If management services are provided by other entities (ie, hospital, accounting, consulting firm)
- The number of staff members to oversee

Table 1-2 provides guidance on selecting the appropriate level of manager for a practice.

TABLE 1-2

General Differences between Managers

	Office Manager	**Practice Manager**	**Practice Administrator**
Education	High school degree, at least some college or a technical degree—sometimes college degree	College degree, often holds a master's degree in business or related field	College degree and master's degree in business or health-related field
Career Track	Has held staff positions (usually in billing and/or bookkeeping) in physician practices for many years; many times is a loyal, long-term employee who can be trusted with confidential issues	Has experience managing other physician group practices, or working in the physician relations department at a hospital; may have some experience in other business industries, too	Has worked for multiple health care organizations (eg, insurance plan, hospital) in addition to a large physician practice; may have held VP-level positions
Level of Managerial Power	Liaison between physician(s) and staff—physician(s) is/are real decision-maker(s)	Empowered decision-maker; works with physicians and incorporates their input before implementation; physicians still lead strategic discussions; obtains board approval for capital expenditures	Empowered, autonomous decision-maker; physicians delegate nearly all but policy and strategic decisions, though the administrator leads these discussions; obtains board approval for capital expenditures
Areas of Expertise	Billing/collections, daily practice operations, personnel issues (eg, vacation schedules, conflict resolution), staff training, bookkeeping	Daily operations, finance, marketing, managed care contracting, information systems, personnel management (eg, hiring, disciplining, performance appraisals)	Finance, marketing, managed care contracting, and network development; managing relationships with external organizations such as the hospital and payers; experience working with a board
Salary Range	$25,000 – $35,000[†] (no performance bonus)	Base: $40,000 – $65,000[†]	Base: $65,000+[†] (plus performance bonus)

[†]Salary range is highly dependent on the region and market. For further information on salary ranges, purchase the Medical Group Management Association's (MGMA) annual salary survey. (Please consult the Resource Section in the back of this book for MGMA contact information.)

Source: Zupko K. Why MD's are disappointed with practice administrators and managers. *The Journal of Medical Practice Management;* 15(5) ©2000 Greenbranch Publishing LLC, 800-933-3711. Used with permission.

LEADERSHIP STYLES

Although there is no cookie-cutter role model of effective medical practice management, there are certain prerequisites that any practice manager should possess. One of the most important prerequisites is knowledge: knowledge of how a medical practice works, how appointment scheduling affects the bottom line, what issues are important to physicians in patient care, and issues of importance in running a business. Managed care, capitation, regulations, and reimbursement are other prerequisites that require expertise and a good working knowledge. Essential knowledge in this area also encompasses how to read and interpret financial statements, how to perform cost analyses, how to compare benchmarks, and how to use data to bring about improvements.

However, knowledge alone does not make a successful manager. The medical practice manager must be able to plan ahead. He or she must be able to gather facts, develop solutions, and then lead the progress toward those objectives according to the plan.

In addition to being able to choose and hire competent people for the positions in the organization, the leader must also be able to direct and motivate those individuals to purposeful action.

Leadership vs. Management

Successful medical practices demand both leadership and management. When evaluating the practice's needs, consider the assessment found in Figure 1-1.

As demonstrated, managers and leaders have very different natures. Some practice managers are indeed managers, while others may be inclined toward the role of leaders. Importantly, each type of personality has definite strengths and weaknesses. Managers are very good at maintaining the status quo and adding stability and order to a culture. However, they may not be as good at instigating change or envisioning the future. Conversely, leaders tend to be very good at stirring people's emotions, raising expectations, and taking them in a new direction. Like other gifted people, leaders can suffer from neuroses and self-absorption.

Most people view leadership as being associated with the role of a *manager;* however, leaders and managers may not be *equal* positions. Leading and managing involve *separate and distinct behaviors and activities.* Leaders and managers vary in their orientation toward goals, conceptions about work, interpersonal style, and self-perceptions.

Managers fulfill four functions: planning, organizing, controlling, and leading. This *leading* aspect of management involves influencing subordinates toward the achievement of organizational goals.

Some people have the capacity to become excellent managers, but not strong leaders. Others have great leadership potential, but for a number of reasons, have great difficulty becoming strong managers. *Both leading and managing are desired aspects in a group situation* for the group to become an efficient and effective body.

FIGURE 1-1

Manager or Leader Self-Assessment Test

Self-Assessment	Yes	No

Are you a manager or a leader? Although often used interchangeably, these two terms, in fact, have very different meanings that represent different personalities, dynamics, and views. By learning whether you are more of a leader or more of a manager, you will gain the insight and self-confidence that comes with knowing more about yourself. The result is greater impact and effectiveness when dealing with others and running your business.

1. Are you a problem solver? Do you focus on goals, resources, or organizational structures to achieve results?

2. Do you tend to focus on current information and react to it?

3. Are you good at reaching compromises and mediating conflicts?

4. Do you prefer working with others?

5. Do you believe in the ideals of responsibility and duty to do a good job?

6. Do you feel deeply tied to your organization's culture?

If you answered yes to four or more of these questions, you are probably more of a manager than a leader. Managers usually emphasize rationality and control and are problem-solvers. Managers tend to be more reactive than leaders because they focus on current information and the job at hand. Leaders, on the other hand, are more inclined to the following traits:

1. Do you visualize a purpose and feel passionately about it?

2. Do you tend to envision and promote your own ideas instead of reacting to current situations?

3. Do you enjoy taking risks?

4. Do you intuitively develop new approaches to long-standing problems or open issues to new options?

5. Do you often find that human relations around you tend to be turbulent or tense?

6. Do you have a sense of self-independence from your work role?

If you answered yes to four or more of these questions, you are more of a leader than a manager. Leaders can visualize a purpose and are often imaginative, passionate, and nonconforming. They can also provide a vision that alters the ways people think about what is desirable, possible, and necessary, and often exhibit a strong dislike for the mundane.

JOB DESCRIPTIONS

Once the management needs have been identified, the practice will be able to move on to the next step, which is to design a job description that will outline the job responsibilities of the manager. The job description should include the position title, to whom the individual reports, a general summary of the position, supervisory responsibilities, education and experience requirements, and performance goals (see Figures 1-2, 1-3, and 1-4 for examples).

FIGURE 1-2

Office Manager Job Description

Office Manager Job Description

POSITION	OVERTIME STATUS	EEO 1
Office Manager	Exempt	Grade P10
REPORTS TO		
Medical Practice Administrator		

SCOPE:

Office manager directs, coordinates, and manages all operations and related activities of a medical practice, which includes organizing office operations and procedures, such as personnel, information management, filing systems, and requisition of supplies, by performing the following duties personally or through subordinate supervisors.

ESSENTIAL DUTIES AND RESPONSIBILITIES:

1. **Patient Care Duties:**
   - Assists medical and clerical staff as needed and cross-trains on clerical responsibilities for continuity of quality patient services.
   - Maintains excellent patient relationships and resolves complaints and nonclinical patient problems.

2. **Supervisory Duties:**
   - Supervises all nonclinical staff.
   - Ensures complete office coverage for all nonclinical duties and assigns duties and coordinates schedules, approves leave.
   - Assists medical practice administrator in developing nonclinical and billing office staffing goals and time benchmarks for meeting goals.
   - Assists medical practice administrator in recruiting, interviewing, and hiring qualified individuals.
   - Resolves all personnel problems and enacts disciplinary actions, in collaboration with medical practice administrator.
   - Establishes meeting schedule and conducts regular meetings with nonclinical and billing office staff.
   - Maintains appropriate and thorough documentation on all personnel actions.

3. **Billing Office Duties:**
   - Performs, assists, and oversees subordinates in performing insurance and patient billing duties.
   - Establishes goals for accounts receivable management and maintains productivity.
   - Prepares composite reports from individual reports of subordinates and submits to finance director on a bi-monthly basis.

4. **Operational Duties:**
   - Manages day-to-day operations of office.
   - Determines work procedures, prepares work schedules, and expedites workflow.
   - Maintains master appointment schedule and calendars for physicians.
   - Ensures office space, building needs, and supplies are provided and maintained appropriately for medical staff and quality patient care.

5. **Quality Assurance Duties:**
   - Adheres to Corporate Compliance Program and serves on Corporate Compliance Committee.
   - Initiates quality review of effectiveness in relation to objectives and costs.
   - Assists medical practice administrator with development of Office Policies and Procedures.

6. **Financial Duties:**
   - Maintains office expenditures, requesting payables according to Office Policies and Procedures and maintains all payable records.

ADDITIONAL SKILLS AND ABILITIES:

Includes the following, but other duties may be assigned:
   - Works as secondary backup for checkout.
   - Assists "management team" during vacations, illness, and backup interviewer.

POSITION	PAGE 2
Office Manager	

ADDITIONAL SKILLS AND ABILITIES (CONT.):
- Performs any and all other duties as required by medical practice administrator to provide optimal patient care.

QUALITATIVE GOALS:
- To coordinate nonclinical services and perform various administrative responsibilities.
- To assist the medical practice administrator with all nonclinical aspects in a timely manner.
- To provide support for all clinical functions with efficiency.
- To demonstrate independence and maturity in decisions.
- To exhibit a positive, motivational, calm, cheerful, caring, and helpful attitude at all times to patients, co-workers and physicians.

QUANTITATIVE GOALS:
- To perform nonclinical patient duties as assigned.
- To implement and oversee nonclinical and billing office staffing goals and maintain collection percentage at 85%.
- To review nonclinical and billing office staffing goals with each staff member every quarter and recommend bonus for all staff achieving collection goal of 85%.
- To conduct meetings with nonclinical and billing office staff every 2 weeks.
- To assist medical practice administrator in establishing and implementing comprehensive Office Policies and Procedures.
- To assist in establishing and implementing Emergency and Safety Policies and Procedures by _____.
- To assist medical practice administrator and ANM in training all nonclinical and billing office staff in Office Policies and Procedures and Emergency and Safety Policies and Procedures by _____.
- To assist finance director in implementing medical supply ordering, inventory, and equipment maintenance procedures by _____.
- To market the practice as needed.

EDUCATION AND/OR EXPERIENCE REQUIREMENTS:
- Associate's degree (AA) or Bachelor's degree (BA) required.
- Minimum 2 years of work experience in a medical office required.
- Minimum 1 year of supervisory experience required.

CERTIFICATES, LICENSES, REGISTRATIONS:
None required.

PHYSICAL DEMANDS:
Work requires sitting, stooping, bending, and stretching for files and supplies. Work requires occasional lifting of files or paper weighing up to 40 pounds. Work requires manual dexterity sufficient to operate a keyboard, calculator, telephone, copier, fax machine, and other such office equipment as necessary. Work requires viewing and typing on computer screens for long periods of time. Hearing must be within the normal range for constant telephone usage and vision must be correctable to 20/20.

The physical demands described here are representative of those that must be met by an employee to successfully perform the essential functions of this job. Reasonable accommodations may be made to enable individuals with disabilities to perform the essential functions.

WORK ENVIRONMENT:
Work is performed in a medical office setting. This employee may encounter the environmental condition of bloodborne pathogen exposure. The majority of time is spent with people. The work environment is oftentimes stressful with multiple tasks. Interaction with people is constant and interruptive. There will be contact with people who are in pain and/or upset. The noise level in the work environment is usually moderate.

FIGURE 1-3

Practice Manager Job Description

Practice Manager Job Description

POSITION	OVERTIME STATUS
Practice Manager	Exempt
REPORTS TO	
Executive Director	

SCOPE:

Under general supervision, provides day-to-day management of a practice's activities and assigned operational areas to ensure accomplishment of its objectives. Assists with the development of practice objectives to ensure financial profitability through short- and long-range planning in order to achieve and maintain growth. Continually evaluates the timely adjustment of practice strategies and plans to meet changing national, state, and local needs.

ESSENTIAL DUTIES AND RESPONSIBILITIES:

- Assists in the development and establishment of policies, procedures, and objectives, and ensures their adequate execution, compliance, and updates.
- Analyzes general and specific business conditions as they relate to operational issues and keeps supervisor fully advised on these matters.
- Assists in developing organizational objectives and plans for their achievement.
- Within scope of authority, oversees the development of systems (both manual and automated) to properly support practice-wide activities based upon business needs. Coordinates hardware and software requirements of existing and future systems.
- Promotes effective communication and adequate information flow within the practice.
- As necessary, delegates portions of activities, responsibilities, and authorities to organization staff, departmental supervisors, and unit supervisors. Ensures that responsibilities, authority, and accountability of all direct subordinates and unit supervisors are defined and understood.
- Ensures all activities are carried out in compliance with organizational policy and local, state, and federal laws and regulations.
- Ensures compensation programs are implemented, administered, and tracked in order to retain a competitively compensated workforce. Ensures adherence to company Human Resources Policy.
- Ensures adherence to legal requirements and government reporting regulations affecting OSHA, EEO, TEFRA, ERISA, and Wage & Hour. Continually monitors exposure of practice. Oversees the preparation of information requested or required for compliance. Submits information to company Human Resources prior to distribution to specific government agencies.
- Ensures the best interests of organization employees in accordance with policies, procedures, and governmental laws and regulations. Recommends probationary actions and terminations.
- Oversees the preparation and maintenance of management reports that are necessary to carry out functions of the practice. Prepares periodic reports as necessary or required.
- Ensures compliance and adherence to the organization's structure, management philosophy, and mission statements.
- Oversees practice compliance with appropriate accreditation body standards.
- Maintains responsibility for all office supervisors and their day-to-day functions.
- Conducts appropriate performance evaluations, and recommends merit increases, promotions, and disciplinary actions.
- Oversees development and coordination of new office locations and their needs as required.

ADDITIONAL SKILLS AND ABILITIES:

- Understands the purposes, organization, and policies of the community's health systems sufficient to interact with other health care providers.
- Understands the policies and procedures of a clinic sufficient to direct its operations and to provide effective patient care.

POSITION	PAGE 2
Practice Manager	

ADDITIONAL SKILLS AND ABILITIES (CONT.):

- Understands the principles and practices of employee development sufficient to ensure organizational productivity.
- Has full knowledge of computer programs and applications.
- Possesses the skills to exercise a high degree of initiative, judgment, discretion, and decision-making to achieve organizational objectives.
- Is capable of accurately analyzing situations and taking effective action.
- Establishes and maintains effective working relationships. Skilled in organizing work, making assignments, and achieving goals and objectives.
- Exercises judgment and discretion in developing, applying, interpreting, and coordinating departmental policies and procedures.
- Organizes and integrates organizational priorities and meets deadlines.
- Has ability to prepare comprehensive reports.

EDUCATION AND/OR EXPERIENCE REQUIREMENTS:

Bachelor's degree (BA) in accounting, finance, or other related business field. Minimum seven (7) years of experience in health care management with at least two (2) years in a supervisory capacity.

CERTIFICATES, LICENSES, REGISTRATIONS:

None required.

PHYSICAL DEMANDS:

The physical demands described here are representative of those that must be met by an employee to successfully perform the essential functions of this job. Reasonable accommodations may be made to enable individuals with disabilities to perform the essential functions. Requires vision and hearing corrected to normal range. Must be able to accurately view computer screen and printed material. Occasionally lifts and carries items weighing up to 40 pounds.

WORK ENVIRONMENT:

The work environment characteristics described here are representative of those an employee encounters while performing the essential functions of this job. Reasonable accommodations may be made to enable individuals with disabilities to perform the essential functions. The work environment is typical of an office setting. Willingness to occasionally travel.

APPROVALS:

Manager/Dept. Head: _____ Date: _____

Chief Administrative Officer: _____ Date: _____

FIGURE 1-4
Practice Administrator Job Description

Practice Administrator Job Description

POSITION	OVERTIME STATUS
Practice Administrator	Exempt
REPORTS TO	
Executive Director	

SCOPE:
Under minimal supervision, provides direction and administration of a practice's activities to ensure accomplishment of its objectives. Recommends practice objectives to ensure financial profitability through short- and long-range planning in order to achieve and maintain growth. Continually evaluates the timely adjustment of practice strategies and plans to meet changing needs.

ESSENTIAL DUTIES AND RESPONSIBILITIES:
- Ensures development and establishment of policies, procedures, and objectives. Ensures their adequate execution, compliance, and updates.
- Evaluates general and specific business conditions as they relate to operational issues and keeps the governing body and the executive director fully advised on these matters.
- Advises and assists in developing organizational objectives and plans for their achievement.
- Undertakes special studies or projects as requested.
- Formulates and implements policies and objectives, both short- and long-range, for activities consistent with company guidelines. Ensures compliance with implementation of policies and objectives.
- Within scope of authority, ensures the development of systems (both manual and automated) to properly support practice-wide activities based upon business need. Directs the coordination of hardware and software requirements of existing and future systems.
- Directs the development and implementation of organizational procedures and controls to promote communication and adequate information flow within the organization.
- As necessary, delegates portions of activities, responsibilities, and authorities to organization staff, departmental supervisors, and unit supervisors. Ensures that responsibilities, authority, and accountability of all direct subordinates and unit supervisors are defined and understood.
- Ensures all activities are carried out in compliance with organizational policy and local, state, and federal laws and regulations.
- Ensures compensation programs are implemented, administered, and tracked in order to retain a competitively compensated workforce. Ensures adherence to company Human Resources Policy.
- Ensures adherence to legal requirements and government reporting regulations affecting OSHA, EEO, TEFRA, ERISA, and Wage & Hour. Continually monitors exposure of the organization. Directs the preparation of information requested or required for compliance. Directs the submission of information to company Human Resources prior to distribution to specific government agencies.
- Ensures the best interests of organization employees in accordance with policies, procedures, and governmental laws and regulations. Recommends probationary actions and terminations.
- Oversees practice compliance with appropriate accreditation body standards.
- Responsible for monitoring, analyzing, assessing, and communicating practice progress. Considers present and planned capacity. In financial terms, considers manpower and practice needs, including facilities and technology. Directs the preparation and maintenance of management reports necessary to carry out functions of practice. Prepares periodic reports as necessary or required.
- Ensures compliance and adherence to the organization's structure, management philosophy, and mission statements.
- Maintains responsibility for all department heads, office supervisors, and support staff.
- Conducts appropriate performance evaluations and recommends merit increases, promotions, and disciplinary actions.
- Attends corporate meetings and related corporate activities.

POSITION	**PAGE 2**
Practice Administrator	

ESSENTIAL DUTIES AND RESPONSIBILITIES (CONT.):
- Oversees development and coordination of new office locations and their needs as required.
- Ensures the coordination of payroll functions and personnel records. Assists with benefits, personnel issues, and special projects as assigned.
- Responsible for petty cash management.

ADDITIONAL SKILLS AND ABILITIES:
- Understands the purposes, organization, and policies of the community's health systems sufficient to interact with other health care providers.
- Understands the policies and procedures of a clinic sufficient to direct its operations and to provide effective patient care.
- Understands the principles and practices of employee development sufficient to ensure organizational productivity.
- Has full knowledge of computer programs and applications.
- Possesses the skills to exercise a high degree of initiative, judgment, discretion, and decision-making to achieve organizational objectives.
- Is capable of accurately analyzing situations and taking effective action.
- Establishes and maintains effective working relationships with employees, policy-making bodies, third-party payers, patients, and the public. Has ability to organize work, making assignments, and achieving goals and objectives.
- Exercises judgment and discretion in developing, applying, interpreting, and coordinating departmental policies and procedures.
- Organizes and integrates organizational priorities and meets deadlines.
- Prepares comprehensive reports.

EDUCATION AND/OR EXPERIENCE REQUIREMENTS:
Bachelor's degree (BA) in accounting, finance, or other related business field. Minimum seven (7) years of experience in health care management with at least two (2) years in a supervisory capacity.

CERTIFICATES, LICENSES, REGISTRATIONS:
None required.

SUPERVISORY RESPONSIBILITIES:
Indirectly supervises department heads and oversees the activities of all clinic and support staff.

PHYSICAL DEMANDS:
The physical demands described here are representative of those that must be met by an employee to successfully perform the essential functions of this job. Reasonable accommodations may be made to enable individuals with disabilities to perform the essential functions. Requires sitting for long periods of time. Some bending and stretching required. Adequate finger dexterity and feeling to perform keyboarding and substantial repetitive motions involving the wrists, hands, and/or fingers. Requires vision and hearing corrected to normal range. Must be able to accurately view computer screen and printed material. Occasionally lifts and carries items weighing up to 40 pounds.

WORK ENVIRONMENT:
The work environment characteristics described here are representative of those an employee encounters while performing the essential functions of this job. Reasonable accommodations may be made to enable individuals with disabilities to perform the essential functions. The work environment is typical of an office setting. Willingness to occasionally travel.

APPROVALS:

Manager/Dept. Head: _____ Date: _____

Chief Administrative Officer: _____ Date: _____

SUMMARY

The requirements of experience, knowledge, and intellect for the role of manager in the medical practice vary greatly, depending upon the size and style of the practice. As the practice grows, the dynamics of management change, often demanding skills in leadership on top of the ability to manage a complex workforce and business entity. The practice must know what is needed in its current stage of business development, and, as the practice grows, it must constantly evaluate the position and the person who is responsible for making it work.

RESOURCES

de Neuville, C. Are Managers Leaders? Available at: http://infotrain. magill.unisa.edu.au. Accessed November 9, 2001.

Zupko, K. Why MD's are disappointed with practice administrators and managers. *The Journal of Medical Practice Management.* March/April 2000; 15, No. 5. Copyright: Greenbranch Publishing, LLC, 1-800-933-3711.

chapter 2

Organizational Structure

Once the practice has defined the level of management it needs, it can develop a practice structure. Structure defines lines of accountability and outlines how people and departments will relate to each other. Structure exists to accomplish the vision of the organization. It plays a vital part in defining the practice.

It is important to look at the following three items when determining which organizational structure to use:

1. The organizational chart itself
2. How the departments and divisions are lined up and how they interact
3. The policies and procedures that govern that structure

THE ORGANIZATIONAL CHART

The most basic organizational chart has all employees reporting to a sole practitioner. Many smaller practices start with an organizational structure similar to the one in Figure 2-1.

This structure is characterized by the focus of all the upward and downward communication to and from the physician. The advantage to this structure is that it can provide the physician with a lot of information about the daily operations of the practice. The lines are simple and direct. However, its disadvantage is that the physician must directly handle all of the staffing problems. The physician is the one making sure that all the contributions fit together, ensuring the smooth operation of the practice.

As the practice grows and the number of employees increases, most physicians find this kind of organizational structure too time consuming. At this point, they usually establish an office manager's position that will act as a buffer between the physician and the staff

FIGURE 2-1

Basic Organizational Chart

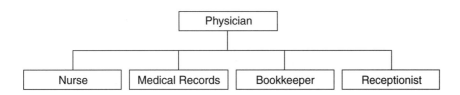

FIGURE 2-2

Organizational Structure with Additional Layer of People

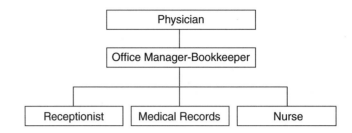

members. The structure, with the additional layer of people, might look something like the one in Figure 2-2.

In this structure, effective communication between the physician and office manager, as well as office manager and staff, is essential. It is also important to hold regular meetings to apprise the physician of what is occurring in the office. This structure can be a benefit for the physician because it removes him or her from the daily operations; however, it can also be detrimental for the same reason. The success of the practice is now partially vested in another person. How that person supports the physician's vision, relates to the staff, and accurately conveys messages to the physicians and staff will have a great effect on the success—or failure—of the organization.

As practices grow and physicians incorporate or form large partnerships, the one physician director structure may no longer be applicable. It is not uncommon to find several physicians in positions of authority. When that happens, practices often form an Executive Committee, which oversees the physicians, manager, and staff. All owners are part of the committee, and the committee directs the workings of the practice. See Figure 2-3.

The advantage to this type of structure is that no one physician has more decision-making authority than the others in directing the practice. The Board of Directors meets (often with the practice manager/administrator) as a whole to make decisions. The manager

FIGURE 2-3

Organizational Structure with Executive Committee

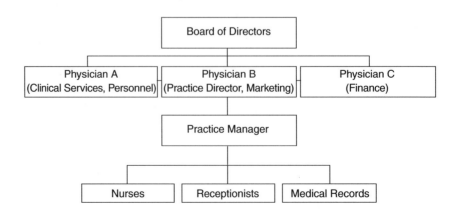

F I G U R E 2-4

Organizational Structure with Practice Administrator Overseeing the "Big Picture"

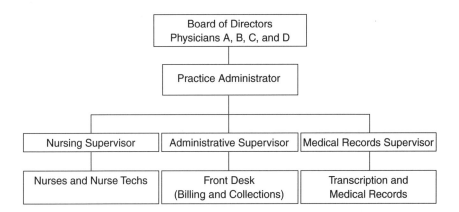

or administrator then takes those decisions and, from them, manages the practice based on the executive decisions. To avoid having to call a meeting each time a decision needs to be made, the physicians are assigned management areas. Usually they are given guidelines regarding the type of decision and the dollar amount they can authorize without going back to the Board for discussion.

In this model, shown in Figure 2-4, the practice administrator oversees the "big picture" of the practice, but responsibilities for staffing are divided among department supervisors.

This structure, which is beginning to resemble that of a larger corporation, has departments, supervisors of those departments, and layers of management. The advantage is that no one person has an overload of direct reports to supervise. As the practice grows, there is really no other efficient method of managing the staff members without dividing the authority among several people. The disadvantage, however, is that as more layers are added, the physicians and even the administrator are even further removed from the daily operations and the thoughts of rank-and-file staff members. The structure begins to resemble a bureaucracy, and decision-making may be slowed and encumbered.

One disadvantage to organizational structures as a whole is that they often exist only on paper and have little effect on the practice. When this happens, staff members who are supposed to be reporting to a supervisor actually report to the practice manager or still directly seek the physicians' decisions. Regardless of which structure is in place, it is important to bear in mind that the purpose of organizational structure is to facilitate communication. If the structure is not supporting good communication, a review of the structure is in order.

SUMMARY

Organizational structures delineate the lines of communication within a medical practice. Generally, smaller practices have more simple organizational structures, but as the practice grows in size (ie, physicians, patient volume, staff members), the practice must transition to an advanced hierarchy for communicating. The challenge is to transfer accurate communication from—and to—the physicians who own the practice to attain the vision of the organization.

RESOURCES

Reeves, CS. *Assessing and Improving Staffing and Organization.* Chicago: AMA Press, 2000.

Winning, EA. *Labor Pains 2002.* Walnut Creek, CA: Winning & Associates, 2002.

chapter 3

Staffing and Human Resource Issues

The ultimate tasks for the physician are finding and hiring the right person for a position within the organization and ensuring that all human resource issues are addressed.

HIRING ONLY THE BEST

When facing any human resource issue, it is important to bear in mind that the primary goal is to build an outstanding team. This means starting with each individual job and achieving the following:

- Hiring the best candidate
- Adding to the candidate's knowledge by offering additional training
- Allowing the candidate to grow in the position
- Developing the candidate to be able to assume a more responsible job
- Providing the candidate with job performance feedback

It is important to begin the process by hiring the best person for the position. This is not achieved through a hurried process or relying on intuition. It is best accomplished by successfully completing each step in the hiring process and by having a written job description for the position that is being filled. The job description can be developed or updated by completing a job analysis worksheet, such as the one shown in Figure 3-1. By completing this job analysis before developing the job description, the manager will gain greater insight into the type of person necessary to successfully fill the position.

Preparing the Job Description

Job descriptions can be prepared in a variety of formats, but they typically include the following elements:

- **Job Title.** The name of the job.
- **Job Summary.** A one- or two-sentence summary that defines the overall function of the job.
- **Job Qualification.** A brief list of educational and experience qualifications needed to perform the job.

FIGURE 3-1

Job Analysis Worksheet

Job Title: _____

Grade/Salary Level: _____

Position Reports to (Title): _____

JOB INFORMATION

List the most important duties and responsibilities (Typically 5 or 6).

_____
_____
_____
_____
_____

Describe the key involvement with others: superiors, subordinates, peers, vendors, customers, or other contacts.

_____
_____
_____
_____
_____

What are the potential sources of satisfaction?

_____
_____
_____
_____
_____

What are the potential sources of dissatisfaction?

_____
_____
_____
_____
_____

What jobs or career opportunities might be available?

_____
_____
_____
_____
_____

Job Title _____
       (as it appears on the organization chart or on personnel records)

Basic Job Function (state in one sentence)

_____
_____
_____

Relationships

Whom does this person report to? _____
Whom does this person supervise? _____
With whom does this person work closely? _____
What are this person's contacts outside the company? _____

FIGURE 3-1
Job Analysis Worksheet (cont'd)

Responsibilities

These will be divided into two groups: primary responsibilities and secondary responsibilities. Condense the tasks you identified into four or five primary responsibilities and four or five secondary responsibilities.

Primary	Secondary

Performance Standards

The performance standards established in the job description will be used in the performance evaluation. The Job Analysis Worksheet will assist in establishing reasonable performance standards. Below are examples of established standards of performance for a receptionist:

1. Answer the telephone within three rings.
2. Identify yourself to caller each time you answer the telephone.
3. Greet patients within 5 seconds of their walking in the door.
4. Process all patient registration with a 98% accuracy rate.

Authority: List authority responsibilities and limits. For example:

1. Can approve purchase up to $500
2. Authority to write off accounts up to $100
3. Has authority to grant time off

- **Duties and Responsibilities.**   A list of major job tasks identifying what is to be accomplished by the employee.
- **Licensing.**   Does the physician prefer an LPN or RN? Will procedures be performed that require some level of licensure (eg, chemotherapy)?
- **Specialized Training.**   An employee hired to perform simple lab tests or X-rays may not require a license, but the proper candidate will need some sort of special training (see sample job descriptions in Figures 3-2, 3-3, and 3-4).

Using Job Descriptions

The job description is a useful management tool that helps promote good employee relations and makes the practice manager's job much easier. When jobs are defined, the practice manager has a handy reference for dealing with many personnel management tasks that arise. The following reasons support the practicality of a job description:

- **Defining job relationships.**   Job descriptions help clarify how each job interacts with other jobs by defining the nature of contacts, authority, and supervision given or received.

F I G U R E   3-2

Medical Assistant Job Description

ABC Practice **Medical Assistant** **Job Description**		
Position		**Overtime Status**
Medical Assistant		Nonexempt
Reports To		
Office Manager		

Scope:
Under direct supervision, maintains efficient patient flow and assists with patient care (ie, vitals, assessments, procedures). Maintains physician's schedule and performs tasks assigned by physicians.

Essential Duties and Responsibilities:
- Escorts patients from the lab to the exam room, the physician's office, or the treatment room as appropriate.
- Records patient data prior to each physician visit, including, but not limited to, vital signs, height, weight, allergies, and medication changes.
- Obtains all necessary patient records as required by physician.
- Assures appropriate consent has been obtained prior to treatment or procedures.
- Conducts patient assessments and obtains pertinent medical information for referral to the physician.
- Directs patients from the exam room or physician's office to the next appropriate station (ie, treatment room, appointment desk).
- Prepares and stocks exam rooms, orders such supplies as needed, and maintains/controls drug samples.
- Assists physicians with exams and procedures as requested.
- Performs EKG and oxymetry readings as needed by physician
- Performs lab procedures and processing of lab specimens as needed. Accurately files all labs and outside reports as needed.
- Obtains blood specimens from peripheral sites as needed and in accordance with OSHA and universal precautions.
- Maintains all exam room disinfection protocols.
- Triages incoming patient telephone calls for referral to nurse or physician.
- Telephones in prescriptions and makes other patient calls as required or directed by physicians.
- Schedules patient tests, procedures, and hospital admissions, and provides follow-up for receipt of test results.
- Arranges for pre-authorizations and pre-certifications as needed.
- Obtains new patient records and previous test results, X-rays, scans, etc.
- Follows up on patient reschedules and no shows with physician.
- Maintains physician's scheduling templates and other miscellaneous appointments and meetings. Advises medical records of physician's absence.
- Maintains a clean work environment and restocks the supply area as needed.

Additional Skills and Abilities:
- Knowledge of medical practice and care to assist in giving patient care. Knowledge of examination, diagnostic, and treatment room procedures.
- Knowledge of medical equipment and instruments to administer patient care. Knowledge of common safety hazards and precautions to establish a safe work environment.
- Ability to assist with a variety of treatments and medications as directed. Skill in taking vital signs, maintaining records, and recording test results.
- Displays excellent verbal and written communication skills.

POSITION	**PAGE 2**
Medical Assistant	

EDUCATION AND/OR EXPERIENCE:
High school graduate or equivalent. Certificate of graduation from an accredited program for medical assistants preferred. Minimum of one year of experience as a medical assistant or nursing assistant in a hospital or clinic setting preferred.

QUALIFICATIONS:
Phlebotomy experience required.

CERTIFICATES, LICENSES, REGISTRATION:
Current CPR certification required.

SUPERVISORY RESPONSIBILITIES:
None

PHYSICAL DEMANDS:
The physical demands described here are representative of those that must be met by an employee to successfully perform the essential functions of this job. Reasonable accommodations may be made to enable individuals with disabilities to perform the essential functions. Requires full range of body motion, including handling and lifting patients, manual and finger dexterity, and eye-hand coordination. Requires standing and walking for extensive periods of time. Occasionally lifts and carries items weighing up to 40 pounds. Requires corrected vision and hearing to normal range.

WORK ENVIRONMENT:
The work environment characteristics described here are representative of those an employee encounters while performing the essential functions of this job. Reasonable accommodations may be made to enable individuals with disabilities to perform the essential functions. Exposure to communicable diseases, toxic substances, ionizing radiation, medical preparations, and other conditions common to a _____(Type of Practice) clinic environment.

APPROVALS:

Manager/Dept. Head: _____   Date: _____

Chief Administrative Officer: _____   Date: _____

- **Training and orientation of new workers.**   The job description provides a ready-made outline to orient the new employee to job responsibilities. Work procedures or job skills training can also be developed based upon the job description.
- **Communication of job responsibilities.**   Throughout the employment relationship, a job description serves as the standard of reference for defining the employee's job responsibilities. A properly prepared job description is the supervisor's best defense against the employee who tries to shirk an assignment by saying, "That's not my job."
- **Recruiting and selecting.**   The job description can be an invaluable aid in recruiting and selecting new employees. Job description details are useful in specifying work qualifications, evaluating resumes or applications, and determining interview questions. According to the Americans with Disabilities Act of 1990 (ADA), an employee's written job description, prepared

FIGURE 3-3

Billing Specialist Job Description

ABC PRACTICE BILLING SPECIALIST JOB DESCRIPTION			
POSITION		**OVERTIME STATUS**	
Billing Specialist		Nonexempt	
REPORTS TO			
Business Office Supervisor			

SCOPE:

Under direct supervision is responsible for all claim submissions, which include verifying accuracy of charges and patient demographic information on claim detail. Responsible for timely follow-up with patients and third-party payers.

ESSENTIAL DUTIES AND RESPONSIBILITIES:

- Collects and reviews all patient insurance information needed to complete the billing process.

- Completes all necessary insurance forms to process the proper billing information in a timely manner as required by all third-party payers.

- Transmits daily all electronic claims to third-party payers. Researches and resolves any electronic claim delays within 24 hours of exception report print date.

- Submits all paper claims and supporting documentation as required by payers. Files all claims, documentation, and other pertinent information in patient financial files.

- Resolves patient complaints and requests regarding insurance billing, and initiates accurate account adjustment. Follows all billing problems to conclusion.

- Resubmits insurance claims as required.

- Maintains confidentially in regards to patient account status and the financial affairs of clinic/corporation.

- Communicates effectively to payers and/or claims clearinghouse to ensure accurate and timely electronically filed claims as per department guidelines.

- Posts all insurance and patient payments within 24 hours of receipt.

- Follows up on collection of patient responsibility portion of bill.

- Submits patient secondary insurance.

- Generates daily, weekly, and monthly reports and forwards to manager.

ADDITIONAL SKILLS AND ABILITIES:

- Knowledge of office procedures. Ability to speak clearly and concisely. Ability to read, understand, and follow oral and written instruction. Basic medical terminology. Knowledge of computerized billing systems.

EDUCATION AND/OR EXPERIENCE:

High school graduate or equivalent. Requires 1 year minimum experience in a medical business office setting.

QUALIFICATIONS:

Familiarity with general billing procedures, preferably in a medical business setting. General computer PC experience preferred.

POSITION	OVERTIME STATUS	PAGE 2
Billing Specialist	Nonexempt	

CERTIFICATES, LICENSES, REGISTRATION:
None

SUPERVISORY RESPONSIBILITIES:
None

PHYSICAL DEMANDS:
The physical demands described here are representative of those that must be met by an employee to successfully perform the essential functions of this job. Reasonable accommodations may be made to enable individuals with disabilities to perform the essential functions. Work may require sitting for long periods of time; also stooping, bending, and stretching for files and supplies. Occasionally lifting files or paper weighing up to 40 pounds. Requires manual dexterity sufficient to operate a keyboard, a calculator, telephone, copier, and other such office equipment. Vision must be correctable to 20/20 and hearing must be in the normal range for telephone contacts. It is necessary to view and type on computer screens for prolonged periods of time.

WORK ENVIRONMENT:
The work environment characteristics described here are representative of those an employee may encounter while performing the essential functions of this job. Reasonable accommodations may be made to enable individuals with disabilities to perform the essential functions. Work is performed in an office environment. Involves frequent interaction with staff, patients, and the public.

APPROVALS:

Manager/Dept. Head: _____   Date: _____

Chief Administrative Officer: _____   Date: _____

---

before advertising or interviewing for the job, is considered evidence of the essential functions of the job. They may be used for determining reasonable accommodation under the ADA.

- **Appraising performance.**   The job description provides a ready list of what tasks the employee should be performing. Referring to the job description, the supervisor can then rate how well the employee performs those assigned tasks.

- **Wage-hour law compliance.**   The job description is an important basis for documenting job responsibilities to classify jobs as exempt from federal and state wage-hour laws. The Fair Labor Standards Act (FLSA), for example, exempts executive, professional, administrative, and outside sales positions from minimum wage, overtime pay, and time-keeping requirements. Nonexempt employees, such as licensed practical nurses, nurse's aides, laboratory technicians or assistants, clerical workers, and the like, are covered by the FLSA.

- **Pay determination.**   Human resource individuals and compensation specialists use job descriptions to determine pay structures and pay ranges for positions. Job descriptions are an important basis for comparing practice pay rates to area salary surveys to assure that pay levels are competitive.

FIGURE 3-4

Patient Service Representative Job Description

ABC PRACTICE PATIENT SERVICE REPRESENTATIVE (PSR) JOB DESCRIPTION	
POSITION	**OVERTIME STATUS**
Patient Service Representative (PSR)	Nonexempt
REPORTS TO	
Office Manager	

SCOPE:

Under direct supervision is responsible for greeting patients and visitors into the clinic in a prompt, courteous, and professional manner. Ensures all appropriate forms are complete, accurate, and signed according to company guidelines. Serves as a liaison between patient and medical staff. Is responsible for scheduling patient appointments and tests in an efficient and timely manner. Answers all incoming calls and directs calls to appropriate personnel.

ESSENTIAL DUTIES AND RESPONSIBILITIES:

- Answers all incoming calls; assesses caller's needs, and directs to appropriate personnel.
- Schedules new patients and return appointments in computer system in accordance with physician and/or office guidelines. Cancels/reschedules appointments according to physician schedule changes and notifies appropriate clinic personnel.
- Maintains physicians' schedule: on call, vacations, meetings, and so forth.
- Greets patients and visitors into the clinic in a prompt, courteous, and professional manner. Obtains all appropriate forms as required.
- Obtains demographic and insurance information. Obtains copy of patient's insurance cards for file. Updates demographic and insurance information as needed in the system.
- Registers all new patients into the system. Prepares and organizes new patient charts. Notifies nursing staff of patient arrivals, placing charts in appointment order. Assists in preparing charts for next days appointments and prints schedules as needed.
- Collects copays, deductible, and other out-of-pocket amounts at time of visit. Issues receipts if necessary.
- Maintains lobby area in a neat and orderly manner.
- Identifies "no shows" and forwards for patient notification.
- Demonstrates an understanding of patient confidentiality to protect the patient and clinic/corporation.
- Follows policies and procedures to contribute to the efficiency of the front office. Covers for other front office functions as requested.
- Demonstrates positive interpersonal relations in dealing with fellow employees, supervisors, other department employees, and physicians so that productivity and positive employee relations are maximized.

ADDITIONAL SKILLS AND ABILITIES:

- Ability to read, understand, and follow oral and written instructions.
- Ability to correctly sort and file materials by alphabetic and numeric systems.
- Ability to courteously deal with patients, co-workers, and insurance personnel.
- Ability to operate a telephone system and utilize appropriate telephone etiquette.
- General knowledge of standard office equipment, such as computers, fax machine, and photo copier.
- General knowledge of medical terminology.
- Ability to clearly and concisely speak. Ability to concisely hear sounds.

EDUCATION AND/OR EXPERIENCE:

High school graduate or equivalent. Five (5) years office experience, preferably in a clinical setting.

POSITION	PAGE 2
Patient Service Representative (PSR)	

CERTIFICATES, LICENSES, REGISTRATION:
None

SUPERVISORY RESPONSIBILITIES:
None

PHYSICAL DEMANDS:
The physical demands described here are representative of those that must be met by an employee to successfully perform the essential functions of this job. Reasonable accommodations may be made to enable individuals with disabilities to perform the essential functions. Work may require sitting for long periods of time; also stooping, bending, and stretching for files and supplies. Occasional lifting of files or paper weighing up to 40 pounds. Requires manual dexterity sufficient to operate a keyboard, a calculator, telephone, copier, and other such office equipment. Vision must be correctable to 20/20 and hearing must be in the normal range for telephone contacts. It is necessary to view and type on computer screens for prolonged periods of time.

WORK ENVIRONMENT:
The work environment characteristics described here are representative of those an employee encounters while performing the essential functions of this job. Reasonable accommodations may be made to enable individuals with disabilities to perform the essential functions. Work is performed in an office environment. Involves contact with patients and public. Occasional pressure due to multiple calls and inquiries.

APPROVALS:

Manager/Dept. Head: _____ Date: _____

Chief Administrative Officer: _____ Date: _____

Create a Candidate Profile

To create a candidate profile, begin with these considerations:

- **Education.** What level of education will the candidate need to successfully handle the job? Will a high school diploma suffice, or will the candidate need an accounting background?

- **Skills.** With which types of office machines should the candidate be familiar? Will computer word processing or spreadsheet experience be required? The training process is reduced if the candidate is familiar with the software programs presently in use.

- **Experience.** What experience is required for the position being filled? Experience with coding, medical terminology, and claims filing are necessary to the insurance billing position, but medical office experience may not be required for a file clerk.

The final step is to periodically review the job process descriptions to reestablish its legitimacy and to ensure the control of the job content. Job content should provide for the following checks and balances:

- **Safeguarding of funds.** For example, not assigning one person to handle all the financial functions, but rather establishing a separation of responsibilities and other duties.

- **Reflect change in workloads and job tasks as the practice grows and changes.** Many times job descriptions are drafted when a practice is established or when a new job is created and not looked at again. Job/process descriptions should be living documents, not static, with modified descriptions to reflect the job as it is today.
- **Increasing employee satisfaction.** As a part of completing the job analysis worksheet, it is important to pay special attention to the "potential sources of satisfaction." If good sources for job satisfaction are not easy to identify, it is time to consider revising the job description. Job satisfaction is high on the list in relation to increasing employee retention and longevity.

Refine the picture of the kind of person desired by considering the following:

- Do we have a clear picture of *exactly* what type of person for which we are looking?
- What will this person have to do?
- What level of experience will the candidate need?
- Are we willing to train?
- How much training are we willing to provide?
- Does the person we hire need to be able to interact with patients or are they away from the action?
- Do they need to be detail-oriented and focused on the task at hand or handle many tasks at once?
- Do they need to display initiative and take the lead or should they just be able to easily take direction?
- Do they need to work with someone who has perfectionist or micro-management tendencies or will they have to manage themselves?
- To develop a precise idea of what we are looking for we will want to assess the following three components of the job:
  - The knowledge, skill, and abilities that are required to do the job
  - The behavior we want to see from the person who holds that position
  - The environmental issues associated with the job

Several recruiting methods are available for finding the most desirable candidates. They include:

- Word of mouth
- Newspapers
- Trade journals and newsletters
- Placement agencies

Each of these methods has its advantages and disadvantages, but the best recruiting strategy often uses a combination of methods.

Place the Advertisement

Advertisements for any position must be carefully written to avoid any appearance of discrimination against gender, age, race, religion, national origin, or disability. The ad should tell enough about the job to interest prospective applicants.

Following are 10 steps to successful ad writing that will attract the right job applicants:

Step 1: Define the job in as specific terms as possible.

Step 2: Include the technical requirements of the job.

Step 3: State hours, days of week, location, travel, and overtime.

Step 4: Express salary range.

Step 5: Describe benefits.

Step 6: State that the practice is an Equal Opportunity Employer.

Step 7: Give information on where to apply (eg, Fax resumes to Attn: Human Resources Department at 555-217-2122 or E-mail to HR@mdoffice.com).

Step 8: Write the ad incorporating all the listed information.

Step 9: Be innovative (ie, the practice's ad must stand out and attract the good candidates).

Step 10: Read the ad as would a candidate seeking employment. What does the ad say about the practice?

Determine which of the candidates to consider by using the following series of qualifier steps:

Step 1: Review the resumes.

Step 2: Conduct a telephone interview.

Step 3: Conduct a personal interview (or interviews).

Step 4: Evaluate the candidate using assessment tools.

Step 5: Check references.

Step 6: Offer "trial workdays."

Resume Review

If the position requires a degree, certificate, license, or specific length of time in a former position, the resume usually provides this information. The resume also reveals if the candidate appears inclined to move frequently from one job to another, to take jobs in different fields for short periods, or to stay with jobs for a substantial period. Beware of false information. According to the cliché, "No one comes so close to perfection as on his resume or job application." The assumption, therefore, is that the only absolutely accurate resume is one that reports no information.

Telephone Interview

Those applicants whose resumes have passed the initial screening will progress to the telephone screening process. By having a set of prepared questions, the interview process is ensured to be fair and the favored answers are not projected onto one candidate over another. Furthermore, this process ensures that each candidate is evaluated with the same criteria.

In the telephone screening interview, a set series of four to six questions is asked of each candidate. Only those who answer "Yes"

FIGURE 3-5

Telephone Interview Questions

Questions	Desired Answers
1. Do you like to work? Why did you leave (or are you leaving) your previous position?	Yes
2. Do other people regularly come to you for advice? (If yes, please give an example.)	Yes
3. Do you do something at work better than anyone else? (If yes, what is it that you do better than anyone else?)	Yes
4. Have you given positive recognition to another person within the past 2 weeks? (If yes, give an example.)	Yes
5. Have you developed enthusiasm in other people within the past 2 weeks? (If yes, how did you develop this enthusiasm?)	Yes
6. Are you considerate of others' feelings? (If yes, please give an example.)	Yes

to all the questions should be considered for a personal interview. By the time the telephone interview process is complete, the field should be narrowed down to two or three good candidates for the personal interview. Figure 3-5 offers a short list of appropriate questions.

Personal Interview

The key to conducting an effective interview is to have the candidate relax, open up, and begin to reveal his or her real character. Therefore, the goal is to conduct the interview in a conversational tone in a relatively informal space that will nurture a sense of mutual trust and respect.

For a good interview, it is important to set aside enough time for an effective meeting and ask that there not be interruptions. The seating arrangement during the interview is as important as the room itself. Interviewing across a desk is like interviewing across a moat. It decreases communication and prevents the conversational tone that promotes comfort and rapport. Chairs placed at right angles will better facilitate conversation and make it appear that the candidate is a "guest" rather than the subject of an interrogation.

If other employees are to be involved in the interview process, it is best to have each one concentrate on a specific area. For example, if the practice is hiring an additional billing or insurance clerk, the incumbent employees should ask questions about coding and billing procedures to determine the candidate's knowledge and skill level.

Active listening is a critical factor in the interviewing process. It is standard to allot at least two-thirds of the interview time to listening. After the candidate has described his or her talents and accomplishments, ask some open-ended questions that relate specifically to the position to be filled.

Here are some examples of questions to ask candidates for a receptionist position:

- How are telephones answered in the current (most recent) job?
- How could this procedure be changed?
- How many incoming lines are currently answered?
- Did the practice have written protocol for answering the telephone?
- What procedure was taken when a patient presented at the reception window?
- Was there a glass window opening to the reception area? Was it kept open or closed?
- When a patient presents at the desk after their visit, what procedure is used?

These questions give valuable insight into the candidate's "people skills." The ability to solicit payment for services is dependent upon an individual's personality and ease of talking with patients.

Also ask a series of questions about the physician for whom the candidate previously worked, such as:

- What medial school did the physician attend?
- Was the physician board certified?
- What services did the practice offer?

Answers to these questions tell how much the candidate knew about the practice and the physicians for which he or she worked. The answers also relay how patients' questions about the practice were answered.

Use the candidate's personal interests to attain insight into personality and learning ability. As an interviewing exercise, provide at least three books with different topics, such as a professional self-help book, a romance novel, and a biography of a famous person and/or a historical novel. Ask the candidate to choose the book they would prefer to read. Ask why it was chosen. There are no wrong choices. Each choice indicates a personality "type." Personality types can be helpful for matching candidates to the position.

If experience and education are equal, a candidate who reads extensively is usually the preferred choice.

Federal discrimination laws also apply to hiring. In seeking information from an applicant, ask:

- Is this a question I would ask either a man or a woman?
- Is this question really needed to judge an applicant's competence or qualifications for the job?

Avoid questions relating to the following areas:

- Age or date of birth
- Sex or race
- Birthplace or national origin
- Religion

- Place of residence
- Arrest and conviction record
- Military service
- Health or disabilities
- Height or weight
- Child care arrangements

Assessment Tools

When using assessment tools, there are three basic options:

- Designing tests
- Purchasing existing tests
- Contracting with an agency to perform the screening

If the practice chooses to design its own assessment tool, all questions should be job related. Devise tests to simulate the actual job the applicant will be doing. Administering assessment tests is legal as long as the tests are conducted fairly and actually pertain to the open position.

Checking References

Before making the final candidate selection for any position, take the time to check references. Letters of reference may provide valuable insight, but they do not take the place of a thorough telephone conference with a prior employer.

Many companies have established a policy of giving only basic information about a past employee. Dates of employment, rate of pay, and the position the employee held is usually all the information that can be gleaned. This is when networking can be beneficial. For example, check with someone who has previously worked with the candidate and ask for an informed reference.

Let the applicant know if satisfactory reference information has been unattainable. If this is the case, ask the applicant for the names of additional references. When checking references, look for the following information:

- References should be current. It is best to contact someone with whom the applicant has worked within the last 12 to 18 months. Rather than calling a reference that employed or worked with an applicant 5 years ago, ask the applicant for more recent references.
- If the applicant does not give a recent employer as a reference, ask for an explanation.
- Friends and family are not considered objective sources.
- Call at least three references.
- Always ask if the employee is eligible for rehire.

Making the Offer

The final phase of the hiring process has been reached. The job offer should be made in writing with a signature line for the new employee to sign, indicating acceptance. Along with the letter should be a job description outlining the position for which the individual is accepting.

All job offer letters should contain the following statement: "This letter is an offer of employment only and does not constitute a contract of any kind." They should also include the start date and the rate of pay on an hourly, weekly, or monthly basis. Do not state the pay on an annual basis. To do so may be viewed as a yearly contract. Indicate the hours that the employee is expected to work and include any benefits that will be provided. Inform the employee of the dress code that is in effect in the practice or if they are expected to wear a uniform.

Do not make any employment promises during the interview or the job offer process. Avoid statements such as:

- Employees cannot be fired without just cause.
- Employees can stay with the company as long as they do their job.
- Employees can expect job security here.
- There are no layoffs in this practice.
- All employees become permanent employees after the probation period.

Once the prospective employee signs the offer letter, a copy should be put into the employee's personnel file. An example of an offer letter is shown in Figure 3-6.

Setting up the Personnel File

Every employee should have a personnel file, including the physicians. Each file should contain the following documents and be appropriately maintained:

- **Personnel file contents.** The typical file should contain all government-mandated forms and employee benefits enrollment forms, as applicable:
  - Resume
  - Employment application
  - Reference checklist
  - W-4 form
  - State income tax form, if applicable
  - I-9 form
  - Payroll set-up form
  - Health insurance enrollment form
  - Long-term disability enrollment form
  - 401(k) enrollment form
  - Flex benefits form
  - Personnel policies acknowledgment form (disclaimer)
  - Attendance records
  - Employment letter
  - Salary change sheet

FIGURE 3-6

Sample Job Offer Letter

Dear_____ ,

Medical Practice Associates is pleased to offer you the position of Medical Assistant. If you accept our employment offer, your effective date of employment will be _____ . Your work hours will be from 8:00 a.m. to 5:00 p.m., Monday through Friday.

Your rate of pay will be _____ per hour. Our pay periods are on the first and fifteenth of each month.

During your first day we will discuss health insurance and other practice benefits, fill out the necessary tax forms, and review your job description.

This letter is an offer of employment only and does not constitute a contract of any kind. The employee and employer agree that the employment is for an indefinite period of time and that either party may terminate the employment at any time and for any reason.

We look forward to your acceptance and having you on our medical team!

Sincerely,

Shirley Bragg
Practice Administrator
Medical Practice Associates

Please indicate your response to this offer by signing and returning this letter by _____

_____   _____

Accepted   Date

- Performance reviews
- Warning or disciplinary letters
- New employee checklist
- Training checklist

■ **Employer access and retention.** Personnel files should be kept in a locked cabinet, accessed only by the designated employee who is responsible for their maintenance.

■ **Employee access.** The employee has the right to access their file at any time, in the presence of a designated employee.

■ **Retention.** The file should be retained for 3 years following termination.

■ **Explanation of benefits (EOBs).**   The health care-related plan is not filed in the personnel file. It is placed in a locked file and may only be accessed by the employee in the presence of a designated employee.

The Orientation Period

Employees will assume "regular" status upon satisfactory completion of the orientation period.

On the first day, present the employee with a copy of *The Employee Handbook*. Take time to explain the basic work rules and regulations, including:

■ Compensation and benefits
■ Payroll deductions
■ Vacation schedules and sick leave
■ Safety and health

Help the employee have a global view of the practice and see how his or her job fits into the overall plan. This explanation will emphasize the importance of the new employee's role and will encourage pride in the job and the practice.

Ask the employee to read *The Employee Handbook*. Offer to answer any questions about policy and procedures. Address any tentative issues, such as dress codes, overtime, and so forth. After the *Handbook* has been reviewed, the employee should sign an acknowledgment form and that form should be placed in the personnel file.

PERFORMANCE APPRAISALS

Performance appraisals are periodic meetings, usually held annually, between each employee and his or her manager or supervisor to discuss the job performance. This is the manager's opportunity to assess each employee's job performance within a specific period. During this period, the manager should be observing how the employee carries out his or her job responsibilities. The manager will be taking note of factors such as how the employee gets along with coworkers, work ethic, promptness, and ability to meet deadlines.

Discipline and counseling should be ongoing and regularly occur. It is not a good idea to wait until the annual performance appraisal to address an employee's misconduct or poor performance. Corrective performance discussions can be scheduled at any time when it becomes necessary to advise the employee of inappropriate or inadequate performance and to specify corrective action. The manager should use this opportunity to outline a program for improved performance and give the employee a time line to show improvement. (Refer to *Disciplinary Action*, page 44.)

Likewise, affirmation of achievement and good performance should also be ongoing to re-enforce favorable work habits, dependability, and achievements. "Thank you" and "good job" are always appropriate—not just during performance appraisal sessions.

Employees are often very tense about a performance appraisal. The practice manager should make the experience as positive as possible. Even if it is necessary to caution an employee about poor performance, it can be done in an encouraging manner. While it is important to point out marginal or poor performance, it is equally important to praise and encourage.

Preparing for the Performance Appraisal

When preparing for the performance appraisal, have all facts in order. Pull out the employee's personnel folder and check for any Corrective Action Forms.

The following information will be useful:

- **Attendance records.**   How many times has the employee been tardy? How many days has he or she been absent?
- **Compliments or complaints.**   Anytime a patient comments about an employee, good or bad, it should be recorded in the personnel record.
- **Disciplinary actions or warning notices.**
- **The job description.**   This is necessary to judge how well the employee is performing each task listed in the job description.
- **Performance goals.**   In previous appraisals or counseling sessions, specific goals for improvement should have been set. Check to see how well the employee has completed these goals.

Performance appraisals, like all other employment decisions, are subject to state and federal labor laws and regulations prohibiting discrimination based on an individual's race, color, religion, sex, national origin, disability, or age. To avoid discrimination, fairly and consistently administer appraisals for all employees. Use the same preprinted form for every employee to assure that the same performance criteria will be used for every appraisal. Figure 3-7 is an example of such a form.

Laws and regulations governing performance appraisals are virtually the same as those that govern the interviewing and hiring of employees.

- Focus on objective, job-related criteria.
- Concentrate on quantity and quality of work and completion of job-related goals.
- Avoid subjective criteria, such as demeanor, bearing, manner, or social behavior.
- Rate good and bad performance.
- Provide a copy to the employee and keep a copy in the personnel record.
- Have the employee sign the performance appraisal. Explain that signing the form does not necessarily indicate agreement with management's findings. However, it does indicate that the employee was informed of the problems. *If the employee refuses to sign the form, indicate this in writing and sign the form.*

FIGURE 3-7
Example Employee Appraisal Form

EMPLOYEE APPRAISAL FORM		
STRICTLY CONFIDENTIAL		Date of this Report:
Employee Name:		Performance Time Period
		From: To:
Department:	Position Title:	
Time in this Classification:		Employment Date:

Instructions:

1. All employees should be appraised at least annually.

2. Use in conjunction with the salary review. Salary changes require approval of the manager and physician.

3. Review employee's work performance for the entire period; refrain from basing judgment on recent events or isolated incidents only.

4. Do not allow personal feelings to govern the rating. Disregard your general impression of the employee.

5. Consider the employee on the basis of the standards expected to be met for the job. Place a check by the area you feel best describes the employee's performance since the last appraisal.

6. Reason must be given for each factor to substantiate area checked.

Quality of Work:

Consider standard of workmanship, accuracy, neatness, skill, thoroughness, economy of materials, organization of job.

❑ Needs much improvement   ❑ Needs improvement   ❑ Satisfactory

❑ Very good   ❑ Outstanding

Reason: _____

_____

_____

Volume of Work:

Consider use of time, the volume of work accomplished, and ability to meet schedules under normal conditions.

❑ Needs much improvement   ❑ Needs improvement   ❑ Satisfactory

❑ Very good   ❑ Outstanding

Reason: _____

_____

_____

Adaptability:

Consider ability to meet changing conditions and situations and the ease with which the employee learns new duties and assignments.

❑ Needs much improvement   ❑ Needs improvement   ❑ Satisfactory

❑ Very good   ❑ Outstanding

Reason: _____

_____

_____

(continued on next page)

FIGURE 3-7

Example Employee Appraisal Form (cont'd)

Judgment:
Consider ability to evaluate relative merit of ideas or facts and arrive at sound conclusions, ability to decide correct course of action when some choice can be made.

❑   Needs much improvement   ❑   Needs improvement   ❑   Satisfactory
❑   Very good   ❑   Outstanding

Reason: _____

_____

_____

Job Knowledge and Skill:
Consider understanding of job procedures and methods, ability to acquire necessary skills, expertise in doing assigned tasks, and utilization of background for job.

❑   Needs much improvement   ❑   Needs improvement   ❑   Satisfactory
❑   Very good   ❑   Outstanding

Reason: _____

_____

_____

Attitude:
Consider cooperation with manager and coworkers, receptiveness to suggestions and constructive criticism, attitude toward practice, and enthusiasm in attempts to improve performance.

❑   Needs much improvement   ❑   Needs improvement   ❑   Satisfactory
❑   Very good   ❑   Outstanding

Reason: _____

_____

_____

Team Effort-Leadership:
Consider ability to inspire teamwork, enthusiasm to work toward a common objective, desire to assume responsibility, and the ability to originate or develop ideas and get things started.

❑   Needs much improvement   ❑   Needs improvement   ❑   Satisfactory
❑   Very good   ❑   Outstanding

Reason: _____

_____

_____

Adherence to Policies and Procedures:
Consider adherence to practice personnel policies and procedures, such as attendance, travel policies, and reporting deadlines.

❑   Needs much improvement   ❑   Needs improvement   ❑   Satisfactory
❑   Very good   ❑   Outstanding

Reason: _____

_____

_____

FIGURE 3-7
Example Employee Appraisal Form (cont'd)

Self-development activities of this employee (to be completed during interview).

_____
_____
_____
_____

PRESENT STATUS, NEEDS, AND PLAN OF ACTION

Overall Effectiveness:
Considering the amount of experience on present job, check the rating that most nearly describes total current performance.

❏ Needs much improvement   ❏ Needs improvement   ❏ Satisfactory

❏ Very good   ❏ Outstanding

What aspects of performance, if not improved, might hinder future development or cause difficulty in present classification (weakness of employee)?

_____
_____
_____
_____

What are greatest strengths of the employee?

_____
_____
_____
_____

Give specific plans you and your employee have made to improve work performance.

_____
_____
_____
_____

Employee Comments:

_____
_____
_____
_____

Forward completed performance appraisal to designated approval authority before reviewing with subject employee. After appraisal is approved, review contents of appraisal with subject employee and complete section concerning specific plans to improve performance. Have employee sign the form and then forward original appraisal to the personnel file. Retain a copy for your files.

FIGURE 3-7

Example Employee Appraisal Form (cont'd)

Performance by Objective

Objectives for:

Use the spaces in the left column to list the most important Performance Management Objectives for the upcoming business year. Include specific business objectives and, as appropriate, one or two personal development objectives. After objectives are determined, the employee and manager should sign and retain a copy of the form. The right column will be used to summarize the employee's performance at year end.

Objectives	Results / Status
1. _____ Completion Date	
2. _____ Completion Date	
3. _____ Completion Date	
4. _____ Completion Date	
5. _____ Completion Date	
6. _____ Completion Date	

Employee comments

Evaluated By:	Title:	Date:
Approved:	Title:	Date:
Employee's Signature (Does not necessarily indicate concurrence)	Title:	Date:

- Document any disciplinary action at the time it occurs. Management's motive in a poor performance discharge may be questioned if the poor performance was not documented at the time of the disciplinary action.
- *Do not avoid poor performance ratings for fear of discrimination charges.* Address performance issues for all employees on a consistent and timely basis.
- Clearly specify a final warning on the Performance Appraisal or Corrective Action Form.
- Avoid backdating appraisals or unusually harsh treatment of the employee to force resignation.
- *Be consistent.* Inconsistency will reflect poorly on any legal proceedings that may arise.
- If poor performance is used to deny or delay a pay adjustment, clearly and thoroughly document this.
- Do not make any discriminatory comments during the performance appraisal or on the appraisal form.

Twenty-Two Tips for Productive Performance Discussions

The following are 22 tips that practices can use during productive performance discussions:

1. **Be prepared.** Define workplace policies and clarify performance standards to achieve a consensus among managers and physicians. Define and use performance-rating definitions. Participate in team performance ratings where administrators or physician rates employee performance. Take some time to be thorough in preparing the performance appraisal form. Complete all parts of the form, including written comments to praise, critique, or clarify a rating. Careful preparation will promote a more meaningful performance discussion.

2. **Plan the discussion.** Carefully plan the discussion with the employee. Use the performance appraisal form as an outline to guide the discussion. Try to anticipate the employee's reaction to the performance ratings. Consider how to respond to the employee's reaction. If daily performance feedback was properly provided during the rating period, there should be no surprises. Rather, the performance discussion will be a review of issues already discussed with the employee.

3. **Get approvals.** Obtain the physician's approval for performance appraisals and any pay adjustments prior to discussion with the employee.

4. **Notify employee.** Notify the employee in advance regarding the performance appraisal discussion. Many practices schedule performance appraisals to coincide with one's employment anniversary or some other designated day of the year. By notifying the employee in advance, more open and positive communications is promoted. Advance notice lets the employee know that preparations have been made to discuss performance and pay issues on a timely basis.

5. **Collect work samples.** Collect any facts, documents, reports, work samples, or other similar items that reflect the employee's job output. These samples will be useful to illustrate the employee's performance, promote objective evaluation of performance, and help to justify performance ratings. Use of work samples focuses discussion to specific job output issues. Be aware of the tendency to generalize overall performance based on a single likable characteristic. Constructive suggestions on how to perform tasks more efficiently help to minimize emotional confrontations.

6. **Allow adequate time.** To have a meaningful discussion, be sure to allow adequate time to discuss job expectations and the employee's performance. As a general guide, performance discussions with employees in more complex jobs, such as skilled, administrative, professional, or management positions, should be 30 to 60 minutes or more. The key factor is to allot sufficient time to discuss job requirements and rate the employee's performance. Suggest ways to improve, and elicit employee response.

7. **Avoid interruptions.**   Pick an interview time and place where interruptions will be minimized or avoided. A private office, conference room, or areas away from the main flow of work are possible locations for performance appraisal discussions. It is disconcerting to have other employees walking by or coming into an office during a performance discussion. Telephone calls also disrupt the performance discussion. Make an effort to prevent or avoid these interruptions. Avoid performance discussions during lunch.

8. **Describe the process.**   By describing the purpose, process, and result of the performance appraisal discussion to the employee, uncertainty is reduced and some of their questions can be answered. Secondly, it helps the manager to take charge of the discussions by defining what issues will be discussed.

9. **Be friendly, yet businesslike.**   The tone of the performance appraisal discussion should be friendly, positive, and businesslike. Avoid joking or nervous laughter during the discussion. Try to encourage the employee to relax. If the employee has serious or continuing performance problems, take a firmer stance to convey the seriousness of the employee's poor performance.

10. **Stay on track.**   Keep to the subject at hand. Do not let the discussion wander into unrelated areas. Thorough preparation will help the manager stick to the discussion of specific performance issues and minimize unrelated discussions.

11. **Follow the appraisal form.**   One easy way to set a direction to the discussion is to follow the performance appraisal form. First, identify the performance factor, then the desired performance norm, and then the rating of the employee's performance. When the results of the employee's work are compared to the expected norm, issues can be discussed on a more objective basis. Avoid personal criticisms or insulting remarks.

12. **Praise achievements.**   Recognition and praise for achievements are important parts of the performance appraisal process. Giving credit, when due, helps the employee to know his or her efforts are recognized. Recognition is an effective motivator.

13. **Identify deficiencies.**   Poor performance must be clearly identified, marked on the performance appraisal form, and discussed with the employee. Be direct. Give specific examples of performance problems and then identify the desired level of performance. The employee will assume that performance is satisfactory unless the problems are specifically identified.

14. **Sandwich technique.**   This technique can be helpful when discussing performance problems. First, compliment the employee on an aspect of good performance, then identify a performance deficiency, and then follow up with another comment about good performance. Clearly, this technique softens the effect of discussing poor performance. Avoid overusing this technique. In cases of serious or repeated poor

performance, be sure to specifically describe the problem and define the desired performance.

15. **Maintain professionalism.** The performance appraisal discussion should be constructive, not confrontational; pleasant and professional, not a contest of personalities; with an element of empathy rather than pitched emotion. Focus on job tasks, results, and accomplishments. Personal attacks on the individual are likely to arouse an argumentative response or result in barriers to communication.

16. **Offer improvement suggestions.** Offer specific suggestions on how to improve performance, particularly when identifying performance problems. Performance improvement is not likely to occur merely by identifying the employee's mistakes. However, performance improvement is more likely when the employee understands proper work techniques and expected performance goals.

17. **Set performance goals.** One key to improved performance is setting performance goals. By defining performance goals, the employee has a target toward which to work. To be effective, goal setting should include employee input. Goals should be achievable with some extra effort. Defined goals provide a ready basis to evaluate performance during the next rating period.

18. **Discuss performance, then pay.** Performance appraisal and pay adjustment discussions may be together. It is best to discuss performance first, and then explain how the performance rating has influenced the pay adjustment. Some employers set these discussions for two separate meetings to maximize each issue.

19. **Don't discredit the practice.** Occasionally, an inexperienced manager may promise a pay raise or tell the employee that management cut a recommended pay raise. When a manager discredits the practice in this fashion, this action really reflects poorly on the manager. Do not fall into this trap.

20. **Encourage employee comments.** A primary objective of the performance appraisal is communication between employees and administrators. Accordingly, encourage all employees to react to the performance ratings. The employee may agree, disagree, or offer reasons (sometimes excuses) for performance problems. Listen to and consider the employee's comments. Allow the employee to suggest ways to improve the efficiency of their position.

21. **Discuss employee goals.** What does the employee want or need in the way of personal development or training? What are his or her future career goals? What additional responsibilities might be added to his or her current position, if any? Is there a possibility of upward mobility?

22. **Employee signature.** Most performance appraisal forms have a space for an employee signature. At the conclusion of the performance appraisal discussion, ask the employee to sign the form. The employee's signature serves to acknowledge that the

performance discussion occurred. Also, many performance appraisal forms have a space for employee comments. In the interest of constructive communication, invite the employee to make written comments.

SALARY ADMINISTRATION

Discussing salary with an employee is a challenging responsibility for the administrator. There are many psychological factors surrounding the employee's perception about pay. A pay increase, or lack of increase, directly affects an employee's self-esteem, morale, and perception of their value to the practice.

Careful preparation for the discussion of pay issues is important to protect the employee's morale and to encourage them to strive to improve, regardless of pay increases. The following tips will help ensure a successful meeting with employees about pay:

- Research the practice's philosophy about pay.
- Obtain approval or discuss the allowed percentage of increase with the physician prior to conducting salary reviews.
- Protect confidentiality. Do not discuss or compare one employee's salary or abilities with another.
- Discuss the relationship between pay and performance.
- Be specific in discussing any performance problems that deny, reduce, or delay a pay adjustment.
- Respond honestly to any questions about pay without violating confidentiality guidelines.
- Take the responsibility to present pay issues to the employee in a way that emphasizes the positive aspects of employment.
- Discuss performance first and pay second.
- Explain how practice conditions, the economy, and practice growth affect pay raises.
- Give the employee a statement of benefits, including insurance, vacation, sick pay, and required government benefits.
- It is critical that reviews be conducted on or very near the date they are due. If the appraisal is delayed for an insignificant reason, it tells the employee that the practice is not concerned about them or their performance.

Because of the ever-increasing cost of operating a medical practice, it is often necessary to explain to employees that finances prevent any pay increases.

Employees should always be made aware of the cost of operations in the practice. Solicit their help and ideas in keeping costs down. Let employees know what steps are being taken to reduce costs. If the employees have been kept in the communication loop, they will not be surprised when it is announced that there will be no raises this year. This announcement may be avoided if the practice has made a concerted effort to save money in other areas.

Emphasize the need for teamwork, cooperation, and continued effort by all employees to get through these tough times. Avoid making promises of future pay raises or commitments about job security. Such promises, if unfulfilled, will further erode morale. *Do not, under any circumstances, discredit the physician for the lack of pay increases!*

Employee perception of pay is a factor in turnover, absences, morale, and motivation. For these reasons, it is important to effectively communicate pay information. For an example of a Salary Change Recommendation Form, see Figure 3-8.

DRESS CODES

Many businesses today are struggling with quandaries about dress codes as the working force leans increasingly toward dressing more casually. Medical offices are no exception. Few practices today

FIGURE 3-8

Salary Change Recommendation Form

SALARY CHANGE RECOMMENDATION

This request is not official until all approvals are indicated and a copy is returned to the manager/supervisor. Complete in duplicate and submit to Payroll Manager.

Date of Request: _____   Date of Employment: _____

Practice: _____

Employee: _____   Department: _____

LAST INCREASE, ANNUALIZED

FROM	TO	AMOUNT OF INCREASE	% OF INCREASE	DATE

PREVIOUS INCREASE, ANNUALIZED

FROM	TO	AMOUNT OF INCREASE	% OF INCREASE	DATE

RECOMMENDATION
SALARY ADJUSTMENT REQUEST – ANNUALIZED

FROM:	AMOUNT OF INCREASE:
TO:	PERCENT OF INCREASE _____ %

TITLE CHANGE: ❏ No ❏ Yes/To: _____

Comments: _____

_____

Signed: _____   Approved: _____
Manager/Supervisor   Administrator

Effective Payroll Date: _____   Approved: _____
Physician

require their clinical staff to wear white uniforms. We see more offices with staff dressed in scrubs (ie, very casual baggy green garb that made its first appearance in operating rooms) as well as uniform tops in multicolored and multipatterned fabrics. Some practices require matching uniforms while others allow individuals to dress according to their own preferences.

The nonclinical staff is often left to its own judgment when it comes to office dress, sometimes with disastrous results. For example, one manager tells the story of hiring a conservatively dressed candidate to fill a vacancy in the nursing department. She thought she had found the perfect person to work with the senior partner and his primarily Medicare-aged patients. When Monday morning came, the newly hired nursing tech arrived with purple hair in a spiked hairstyle. Despite the trend toward more relaxed apparel, medical practices are still medical practices and patients expect a degree of conservatism and professionalism when they visit their physician's office. To avoid surprises (eg, purple hair, bare midriffs, barely-there skirts), dress policies need to be established and communicated to all current employees as well as employment candidates.

For example, a dress policy that stresses comfort and safety while maintaining a professional decorum may be similar to those below:

Female staff: Dresses skirts and blouses, slacks and blouses/ sweaters. Comfortable, low-heel shoes are acceptable. Unacceptable wear includes: culottes, skorts, low-cut shirts and blouses, bare midriffs, low-cut slacks, shorts, cutoff shorts, sandals, tennis shoes, jeans or denim attire, visible facial body piercing (other than ears), and visible tattoos.

Male staff: Shirts, slacks, and ties are mandatory. Hair, including beards and mustaches, should be neatly trimmed and clean. Unacceptable wear includes: shorts, low-cut slacks, cutoff shorts, sandals, athletic shoes, jeans or denim attire, visible facial body piercing (other than ears), and visible tattoos.

Other: For those who deal directly with patients, smocks or lab coats are acceptable. Uniforms may be required and this may be identical uniforms or within a specified range, such as white slacks with uniform shirts in specified colors or design.

As a word of caution, many state laws specify that when a company requires its employees to wear uniforms, the employer is responsible for the cost and upkeep of those uniforms. Before mandating uniforms for clinical or entire office staff, check with state laws to determine financial responsibility.

DISCIPLINARY ACTION

Disciplinary action can be taken against an employee for a number of reasons, including performance, misconduct, or similar problems. Sometimes these issues can be resolved amicably; however, sometimes they result in the termination of the employee.

Performance Problems

A *performance problem* is generally defined as an action or inaction that causes work tasks to be performed poorly or in a manner that fails to meet expectations. Errors in completion of reports or data, inability to complete tasks on time, and failure to meet standards for quality and quantity of work are all examples of poor performance.

The administrator should address performance problems as soon as they become apparent. Any employee can have a bad day or a bad week. However, a counseling session is in order if poor performance continues for more than a few days.

In order to fairly judge if an employee is performing up to expectations, there must be guidelines for performance, such as a job description.

Thoroughly explain to the employee the areas of the poor performance. Outline specific instructions for how the performance should be improved. Give a definite time line for improvement. Set a specific date for another meeting to discuss progress. Above all, stick to the time line and monitor progress daily.

Document all corrective action. Obtain the employee's signature on the *Corrective Action Form* and place a copy in the employee's personnel file.

Misconduct Problems

Misconduct is defined as *a violation of policy or published rules.* Common examples may include theft, insubordination, use of drugs or alcohol, or excessive absenteeism.

Refer to the practice's *Employee Handbook* when addressing a misconduct incident with an employee. Disciplinary action for misconduct commonly takes the form of verbal warnings, written warnings, suspension without pay, and, ultimately, discharge.

If the warning is verbal, record the date of the warning and a brief description of the infraction in the employee's personnel record. For example:

> June 25, 2001. Maryann was warned about her absenteeism today.
> (Signature.)

If preferable, two verbal warnings may be given before a written Corrective Action Form (see Figure 3-9) is completed. The disciplinary process should be described in *The Employee Handbook* and the guidelines followed exactly for every case of poor performance or misconduct.

Other corrective action tips:

- Investigate the incident
- Verify facts, check records, and get statements from "witnesses"
- Speak with the employee in private
- Specify the nature of the misconduct and why it is inappropriate
- Specify what corrective action must be taken
- Specify what happens if the misconduct continues (ie, suspension, termination)

FIGURE 3-9

Example Corrective Action Form

CORRECTIVE ACTION FORM

Employee's Name: _____

Job Title: _____   Division: _____

Hire Date: _____

TYPE OF ACTION: (Check One)

❏ Verbal Warning   ❏ Final Warning   ❏ Discharge

❏ Written Warning   ❏ Disciplinary Suspension

I.   **Incident:** Describe the situation (eg, behavior, performance, policy violation) that occurred. Include date(s), time(s), people involved, witnesses, effects of incident on employee's work or other employees, and all other relevant circumstances or contributing factors. Please be specific in stating observable behaviors and comments wherever possible.

_____

_____

_____

_____

_____

_____

_____

_____

_____

II.   **Goals and Time Frame for Improvement:** What specific actions, within what time frame, are to be accomplished to improve the behavior/performance?

_____

_____

_____

_____

_____

_____

_____

_____

III.   **Follow-Up Review Date:**

IV.   **Consequences:** What will happen if employee fails to meet the goals set within the designated time frames?

_____

_____

_____

_____

_____

_____

_____

_____

Example Corrective Action Form (cont'd.)

V. Employee's Comments: My manager has reviewed the above situation with me and my comments are as follows:

_____

_____

_____

_____

_____

_____

_____

_____

_____

_____

Manager's Signature: _____ Date: _____

I understand that my signature indicates that this incident has been reviewed with me and does not indicate agreement or disagreement with the action taken.

Employee's Signature: _____ Date: _____
(not required for verbal warning)

The most important factor in dealing with disciplinary problems is to document the incident and assure that the documentation is factual and complete.

Termination

Employment-related/work-related lawsuits have skyrocketed throughout the years as a result of a litigious culture. Increases in litigation, combined with the fact that recruiting and training a new employee is expensive and time-consuming, tend to deter employers from discharging unsuitable employees often enough or soon enough. When a great deal of money and effort are spent on employees that are not producing, the productive employees feel cheated.

Here are seven steps to a legal termination process:

1. **Act on problems immediately.**   Employees most likely to sue are those who think they have been unjustly fired. Immediately communicate with them about poor performance and track their improvement, if any, through weekly or monthly sessions.

2. **Document thoroughly.**   Use written Corrective Action Forms and conduct regular performance appraisals. Be specific in describing an incidence of poor performance or misconduct. Make sure there is documentation of every session with an employee.

3. **Include the employee.**   Have the employees evaluate themselves. If problems are acknowledged, resolutions are more

likely to be found. If they are denied, the employer may have the necessary ammunition in court that the employee did not respond to constructive criticism.

4. **Act quickly.**   If the employee's performance does not improve after counseling, do not delay the decision. There is no **legal** reason why disciplinary actions must be documented, but the practice's policy must be followed. Avoid claims of discrimination by having the documentation for the issue of termination.

5. **Be candid.**   Explain to the employee the reason for the termination. Have someone else present from the practice to witness and record the termination and the employee's responses.

6. **Prepare a Termination Checklist.**   Collect any keys or materials from the employee that belong to the practice. Have the employee's final check ready. If the employee has insurance through the practice, explain the COBRA benefits. (See Chapter 6, *Consolidated Omnibus Budget Reconciliation Act of 1985 (COBRA)*, page 74 for further information, and review Figure 3-10.)

7. **Reassure other employees.**   When an employee is terminated, it may affect the morale of the other employees. They may feel like they will be next. Take the time to explain what happened and explain that there are no plans to fire anyone else.

THE EMPLOYEE HANDBOOK

The Employee Handbook may be one of the most useful tools in a practice. It provides the employee with a written guide to practice policy and benefits. It also helps the manager by furnishing a reference for fair and impartial administration of policies and benefits. With practice policies, work rules, and benefits in writing, many complaints and misunderstandings can be quickly and easily addressed. Written policies reduce the risk of a lawsuit by a disgruntled employee who feels unfairly treated or unjustly discharged. One word of caution: Place an "employment at will" disclaimer in a prominent place in the handbook to avoid the handbook serving as an employment contract.

Writing an employee handbook is a significant undertaking. Begin by considering what the practice would like the staff to understand. A well-written handbook will answer the following questions:

- What is expected of the employee and the employer?
- What are the policies on wages, working conditions, and benefits?
- What services does the practice provide to patients?

Use the handbook to express the following:

- The philosophy of the physician and the mission of the practice
- A sense of security and belonging for the employees

FIGURE 3-10

Terminating an Employee Checklist

TERMINATING EMPLOYEE CHECKLIST		
Employee: _____ **Date of Termination:** _____		
Action	**Responsibility**	**✓**
Keys Returned	Manager	
DOL State of Separation Notice	Manager	
Termination Date to Payroll Manager	Manager	
Termination Information (eg, salary, vacation) to Payroll Manager	Manager	
Termination Letter		
Termination Memo to Staff	Manager	
Removal from Employee Roster		
Exit Interview Letter		
COBRA Form (for continuation of insurance)		
Exit Interview Letter Sent		
401(k) Plan		
Defined Benefit Plan		

- What the employer expects of the employee
- What the employer provides the employee
- How to get help with problems and information on benefits

By preparing an employee handbook, the manager is able to reexamine practice policies and create a level of understanding between managers and employees. It can be beneficial to allow employees to participate in the process of creating the handbook, thus bettering communication within the practice. The handbook can set the framework for successful relationships between the employer and employees by identifying conditions of employment, what employers need to know to satisfy those conditions, and what assistance the practice will provide in meeting those conditions.

A handbook should be attractive and easy to use. Select a size that is neither too large nor too small. Typical sizes are 3″ × 6″ or 5″ × 7″. Loose-leaf binders allow for replacement of pages when policies or benefits change. Policy statements in handbooks should be general enough that they do not require frequent changes.

For ease in reading, follow these pointers:

- Limit the use of words with three or more syllables.
- Keep each sentence to 20 words or less.
- Limit discussion of a subject to one page.
- Use drawings, charts, and cartoons where applicable.
- Leave at least one-quarter of each page blank.
- Limit the number of pages (convey a simple message).

Choose a writing style and be consistent throughout. Use "you" and "your" if a personal style is desired. Or, approach policies in a general way by using an impersonal style. Another effective approach is to ask a question in the heading and then answer the question in the discussion below the heading.

Write clearly and concisely. Use gender-neutral terminology. Avoid gender-based pronouns and expressions wherever possible. If writing is difficult, get outside help with composition, grammar, or style.

Include in the handbook what employees need to know to get along on the job. Working hours, dress codes and standards, break periods, paydays, absences, safety, and general information about the working environment should be addressed. The handbook should also describe what the practice offers in benefits and special services, such as vacations, leaves, medical benefits, jury duty, holidays, educational assistance, and insurance. Typically, the handbook also contains a welcome message, a short history of the practice, and a disclaimer statement. Arrange the content by sections, such as: (1) welcome and introduction, (2) employment policies and procedures, (3) benefits provided, (4) safety, (5) employee conduct and disciplinary action, and (6) summary and acknowledgments. Use of a table of contents is helpful.

Handbooks vary due to individual needs and circumstances. Figure 3-11 shows a sample table of contents can be used as a checklist for deciding what to include in your handbook.

Sample Table of Contents for Employee Handbook

1. **Welcome Letter and Introduction**
   - Letter of Appreciation to Current Employees
   - Letter of Welcome to New Employees
   - Purpose of Handbook
   - Background of Practice
   - Organization Chart
   - Physician(s) Biographical Information, and so forth
   - Equal Employment Opportunity Statement
   - Suggestion and Complaint Procedures

2. **Employment Policies and Procedures**
   - Nature of Employment
   - Probationary Period
   - Employee Relations
   - Supervisor's Responsibilities
   - Employee's Role and Responsibilities
   - Work Schedules
   - Rest and Meal Periods
   - Overtime Policy
   - Attendance and Punctuality
   - Time Cards/Records
   - Personnel Records
   - Payday
   - Payroll Deductions
   - Performance and Salary Reviews
   - Resignation/Termination
   - Telephone Use

3. **Benefits**
   - Holidays
   - Vacations
   - Hospital and Medical Insurance
   - Life Insurance
   - Pension and Profit-Sharing
   - Training
   - Educational Assistance Program
   - Service Awards
   - Workers' Compensation
   - Sick Leave
   - Disability Leave
   - Personal Leave
   - Bereavement Leave
   - Jury Duty
   - Witness Duty

4. **Safety**
   - Safety Rules
   - Emergency Procedures
   - Personal Protective Equipment
   - Reporting Accidents

(continued on next page)

FIGURE 3-11

Sample Table of Contents for Employee Handbook (cont'd.)

5. **Employee Conduct and Disciplinary Action**
   - Standards of Conduct
   - Confidentiality Policy
   - Smoking Policy
   - Drug, Alcohol, and Substance Abuse Policy
   - Sexual and Other Forms of Impermissible Harassment
   - Security Inspections
   - Solicitation
   - Personal Appearance Standards
   - Dress Code
   - Corrective Discipline Procedures

6. **Summary and Acknowledgment**
   - Disclaimer Statement

SUMMARY

Addressing staffing and human resource issues is one of the primary functions of practice management. Identifying and selecting suitable candidates, and hiring and training them are just the beginning of the practice manager's responsibilities. Keeping the work ongoing through satisfied, motivated, and compliant staff members is quite time consuming and can be immensely challenging. The manager who hires and manages the staff through systematic plans, established procedures, and written processes will meet that challenge.

chapter 4

Training and Education

Every medical office needs a staff training plan. Even if the policy is to only hire highly experienced workers or to retain its staff without any turnover for many years, there will be times that training and education are necessary. Most practices find that they need to develop staff training programs to train new personnel because it is difficult to find people with the required skills set, to focus on quality improvement and efficiencies, or to be used as a motivator to reward and retain staff members. Along with the awareness that such staff training programs are necessary, comes the inevitable questions about the type of programs that are needed. For example: What training will new staff members need? How in-depth should the orientation process be? How do we provide continuing education for our existing staff? How do we know that training dollars have been well spent?

Experts in staff training and development have identified three critical times at which it is necessary to provide training:

1. **When the staff member is first hired.** The practice can provide a developed orientation program within the practice.
2. **When there are new developments in the field.** This can be as a result of new technology, such as new medical equipment or new computer system; or when there is a change in regulations, such as has been experienced in recent years with Medicare, Medicaid, HIPAA, and OSHA regulations.
3. **When an individual assumes new responsibilities.** That can be as a result of a change in a position within the organization, of cross-training purposes, or for those practices that hire the untrained worker and are willing to train them to do the job at hand.

ORIENTATION

Orientation to the practice should be part of the hiring process. The practice should develop a formal and structured orientation program that outlines what the staff member is to know before being able to move on to the next step. The orientation should include:

- Review of rights and benefits
- Compliance issues, such as OSHA compliance plan, sexual harassment, and hostile workplace issues

- The organization's policies regarding patient confidentiality
- Review of the mission

The orientation should also include information about the practice itself, including:

- How long has the practice been in existence; the physician's education, specialty, and schedules; services provided; and satellite locations.
- Information about the facility. How to work the telecommunications equipment, where staff members are permitted to park, security issues, computer passwords, copying, and telefaxing policies.

Once the staff member has received a formal orientation, it is advisable to provide him or her with a written or oral test. By completing the test, the employee can prove his or her retention of the information and the employer has proof of the new employee's knowledge if future breaches should occur (eg, not calling in when sick). With such written confirmation, discipline can be forthcoming without the added concern that the staff member was not aware of the rule or regulation. Once new staff members have been introduced to the practice's policies and information in the orientation program, they can become full-fledged staff members. For a more in-depth look at a typical orientation process, review Figure 4-1.

This orientation process can be spread out over several days or weeks depending upon the size and structure of the organization. The second time staff members will need to have training or education is when there are new developments in the field. This can be when new technology is designed to perform current functions, such as when a new computer system is implemented, an electronic medical records (EMR) conversion is introduced, or a new medical instrument is purchased.

NEW DEVELOPMENTS IN THE FIELD

Training is also required when new regulations or developments are identified in the field. This can pertain to Medicare or Medicaid issues, the Health Insurance Portability and Accountability Act (HIPAA) and compliance, CPT ICD-9 coding, or JCAHO certification. When training staff members on the new developments in the field, some important issues must be considered. First, training must be timed so that the newly learned skills can be directly carried over into the job because the use of these new skills increases the retention of knowledge. Furthermore, the practice may want to use the "train-the-trainer approach," where one person is sent for formalized training and then returns to the practice to educate the rest of the staff members on the topic.

Other methods of obtaining this type of training are to have a trainer come to the office, such as when a new computer or instrument is purchased. Usually some training is offered when a new instrument, computer, or EMR system is purchased. This can be

FIGURE 4-1
Orientation Checklist

Topic	Orientation completed by	Date
Information About the Practice		
History of the organization		
Biographical sketches of physicians and their areas of expertise		
Mission and value of the practice		
Number of employees and locations of other offices		
Organizational chart and reporting lines that describe the practice structure		
What level of service do you expect for your patients		
Information About the Working Environment		
Tour of facility		
Types of correspondence and approval for each (eg, memo, E-mail)		
Dress code		
Identification badge, building pass, parking pass		
Policy for entering the building after hours		
Security and safety issues		
Refrigerator policies		
Selling of fund-raising or other goods		
Information Handbook		
Personnel policies		
OSHA training		
Hazardous communication training		
Compliance training		
Release of confidential information		

negotiated in the purchase price, but it may also be well worth the extra dollars spent to have someone from the technology company come and train or retrain the staff as needed.

A second reason to obtain staff training is when there are new regulations that affect all medical practices. It may be beneficial to find staff training resources through a medical society, local hospital, audio conferences, or web-based training to offset the cost.

The third reason to provide training is when a staff member assumes new responsibilities. This may be when staff members are newly hired, when they assume new responsibilities, or when the practice has agreed to hire inexperienced workers and train them. In situations such as this, reference manuals and job aids can facilitate training and make the process easier and faster. There are several different types of manuals (eg, the reference manual, user's guide, tutorial technical manual, online documentation).

WHEN AN EMPLOYEE ASSUMES NEW RESPONSIBILITIES

There will be many times throughout a staff member's tenure with an organization that the person will have to be trained on how the job is done, including the first few days on the job or when an employee assumes a new responsibility. This is true for employees who have considerable background experience, as well as those who are fairly new to the work environment.

When conducting this in-house staff training, the key to its success is to have the right person perform the training. Just because some employees can competently perform their jobs does not necessarily mean they will make adequate trainers or teachers. The steps in providing training for a new employee are:

1. Explain the importance of the task that is about to be described. For example,

    > It is very important to get this demographic information correctly entered into the computer because this is what ultimately is submitted to the insurance carrier. Innocent errors on the front end when capturing this information can result in possible fraud or abuse issues if the errors repeatedly occur.

    Once the employee understands the importance of learning how to correctly do the job, the trainer should then move to Step 2.

2. Demonstrate how to correctly do the job.

3. Have the trainee demonstrate to the trainer that they can correctly do the job.

4. Coach the employee on ways to improve performance of the job.

Once the individuals have demonstrated proficiency, they should be given a certificate. This should be tracked in the employee training record so that if at a later time the employee fails to perform the task according to the standard protocol, there is evidence that the employee was actually trained and could correctly do the job. This is not to say, of course, that the staff member will not forget at first how to do that job or that he or she will not need additional coaching in the first few days on that job. What it does mean though, is once that employee is considered trained, the employee must understand that he or she is expected to do the job the way he or she as trained. It is very important for a practice manager to be able to tell the difference between a training issue and a behavioral issue. Training issues are involved when the employee has never really grasped the idea or learned to do the job correctly. However, behavioral issues can be identified for those employees who have actually demonstrated that they can correctly do the job, but choose not to do so.

TRAINING AIDS

The reference manuals are often known as the last word or ultimate word in an office. These can be alphabetically organized by function or segment. Examples of reference manuals are personnel policy manuals, billing policy manuals, OSHA manuals, and other protocol manuals. These are excellent resources as long as someone is responsible for keeping them up-to-date.

Tutorials are usually used for step-by-step sequencing subtasks and steps. Tutorials are usually used for assisting staff members in operating computer systems, telephone or switchboard system, and physical equipment.

A job aid is an item that stores information externally for the user (Figure 4-2). It guides the user to correctly perform the task, and is used during the actual performance of a task. Job aids are timely because they can be effective in reducing error rates and increasing productivity. They are less expensive than formal training classes and can help transfer to the job what the person has learned in formal training.

ONGOING TRAINING

The more formalized the ongoing training program of a practice, the more inclined the training is to be done on a regular basis. Ongoing training can include coaching sessions held one morning a week, a huddle at the beginning of each day, regular staff meetings that provide an educational component, internal newsletters, bulletin boards, and practice-based intranet can all provide updates and ongoing training for staff members.

FIGURE 4-2

Job Aids—Creating Quick Reference Guides

Job Aids—Creating Quick Reference Guides

How many times have you had to train staff members to perform an ordinary, but infrequent, assignment? For example, how often have you had to refer to the "instruction card" to refresh yourself on how to perform a task, such as resetting your VCR or performing the backup on your computer?

When it comes to performing certain responsibilities, you can save time and help prevent errors by creating job aids. A job aid is a quick reference guide that outlines the steps necessary to complete a task that is not performed frequently or is very complex.

The job aid may be in the form of a step-by-step guide, a worksheet, a checklist, or a flowchart. In developing a job aid, consider the following:

1. Include only the steps necessary to perform the function.
2. Keep the information simple.
3. Use language that the user will understand. Use verbs and action words at the beginning of the sentences.
4. Use drawings or graphics, when appropriate, to clarify information.
5. Be sure the aid is accessible and convenient to use.

Bear in mind that when measuring the effectiveness of job aids, results do not always have to be measured in dollars. Increased patient satisfaction and error reduction can become a basis for improving overall practice performance.

Source: Adapted from *ASTD Info Line*, Create Effective Job Aids, American Society for Training and Development, Alexandria, VA. Available at: www.astd.org.

SUMMARY

Training and educating medical office staff continues to be an ongoing area of concern. Physicians and managers who accept the fact that they will need to provide training to their staff members and budget the time and resources for accomplishing this task will reap the benefits of happier employees. Unskilled or untrained staff members cause errors and extra work for other employees, which can lead to poor morale, lack of teamwork, and a breakdown of office functions. The practice that takes training seriously will improve efficiency.

RESOURCES

Aho, KL, Frantzreb, RB. *Be a Better Job Analyst.* Alexandria, Va: American Society for Training and Development; March 1989.

American Society for Training and Development. ASTD Info. Line: Create Effective Job Aides. Available at: www.astd.org.

Thorne K, Machray, A. *Training on a Shoestring.* London: Kogan Page Ltd; 1998.

chapter 5

Managing Staff/Team Building

Successful medical practice management relies heavily on the practice manager's skills and applications in relation to team building, conflict management, motivation, communication, and the capacity to induce change.

TEAM BUILDING

The traditional definition of a team is a group of people who share responsibility for the decisions that affect them all. Teamwork means contribution and collaboration. It requires both the freedom and the ability to fully participate.

Building a successful medical staff team requires listening, asking for ideas, and communicating the practice's goals to the employees.

Benefits of Teamwork

Teamwork benefits the medical practice in several ways, including the following:

- A smoothly functioning team better serves the patient.
- Members of a smoothly functioning team experience greater job satisfaction.
- A smoothly functioning team reduces the risk of malpractice.

Teamwork is most likely achieved through impartial management. Factions may tend to develop between clinical and front office personnel and between front desk staff and the billing office—a tendency that must be guarded against. Encourage the physicians and clinical personnel to interact more with the front office staff. Have front desk staff and billing personnel meet on a regular basis. Sometimes, saying "thank you" at the end of the day is all that is required.

Cross-training encourages teamwork. Medical assistants can be trained to answer the telephones, use the computer, check in a patient, make an appointment, and file charts. Administrative employees should be capable of taking vital signs, chaperoning a patient to an exam room, scheduling a lab test or surgery, and preparing an exam room for the next patient.

By working closely together to understand each other's needs, both the clinical and administrative staff will develop an appreciation for the problems that exist on both sides of that *invisible line* that seems to exist between the clinical and administrative personnel. For a fully functioning team to operate smoothly, employees must understand their own roles and how their roles interact with and affect others. Cross-training encourages this understanding.

Managing Conflict

Conflict occurs in every workplace. Clashes occur among staff members and with patients when misunderstandings or differences arise. Managing conflict requires a great deal of patience, understanding, and finesse. Conflict should not be suppressed, nor should it be allowed to escalate to open clashes. In effective teams, disagreement is perceived as healthy and is handled by promoting open discussion on the topic. The administrator's role is to make the team responsible for solving problems. As soon as the administrator says, "I'll take care of it," other parties feel absolved from the responsibility of resolving the conflict instead of working through the issues themselves.

The principles for resolving conflict relate to all human interaction. These principles can be used when dealing with conflicts between staff members, as well as clashes between staff members and patients. Knowledge and understanding of the hostility cycle will permit interaction with the individual without escalation of the conflict. Figure 5-1 shows the steps to take at each stage to reach a satisfactory resolution.

The steps to take to resolve conflict include: (1) take-off stage, (2) slow down, (3) accepting of support, (4) cool off, and (5) problem solved. These steps are discussed in detail in the following list

1. **Take-off stage**
   - **Stay calm.** Most medical practices are high-pressured environments that can foster short tempers. When a patient approaches a practice employee with a problem, it is important to remain calm and not become defensive.
   - **Listen.** Even if it is an interruption, it is extremely important to the patient that whomever he or she is addressing, stop and listen. Make eye contact and move closer to let them know that their issue is of interest. Be sensitive to what the patient is feeling and communicate empathy with facial expressions and by nodding occasionally (ie, "I understand").

FIGURE 5-1

The Hostility Cycle

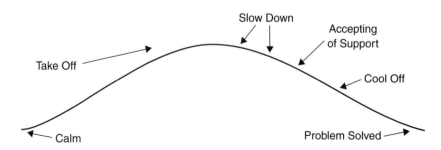

■ **Let out emotion.** Allow the patient to vent his or her feelings. Trying to prevent this will often compromise the process and fuel the patient's frustration.

2. **Slow down**
■ **Take responsibility.** Do not hand off the problem to someone else before allowing the patient to speak. Respond by offering to get the attention of the appropriate person to handle the problem.
■ **Ask questions.** Using open-ended questions that begin with who, what, why, where, when, and how will engage the patient in a more civil discussion and will slow down emotions.
■ **Confirm.** Restating the problem will reassure and confirm to the patient that the issue is understood.

3. **Accepting of support**
■ **Take action.** If possible, demonstrate to the patient that action has been taken. Write down notes and make telephone calls with the patient present to show that the problem has been taken seriously and the wheels have been set in motion.

4. **Cool off**
■ **Make a plan.** Offer alternatives and arrive at a solution. Keep the commitment and follow up on the resolution, especially if it was delegated to a coworker to handle.

5. **Problem Solved**
■ **Exceed expectations.** Be honest and let the patient know exactly what to expect. Do not promise more than can be delivered. If possible, exceed expectations by returning the answer sooner. Try to not give a specific time that the problem will be resolved unless a specific date of delivery can be set. In addition, calling the patient by name will demonstrate that a personal interest in them has been taken. It is difficult for a patient to stay angry once they see concern.
■ **Thank you.** When appropriate, thank the patient for bringing the problem to the practice's attention.

Motivating Employees—What Do They Really Want?

Motivation can be extrinsic or intrinsic. *Extrinsic factors* are intangible (eg, consistent recognition, praise) and are usually inducements to comply with organizational requirements. Research suggests that the heavier the use of extrinsic factors to induce behavioral change, the more difficult it is to achieve a long-term culture change. Getting employee input about rewards can give the organization valuable feedback about employee beliefs.

Some ideas for developing *intrinsic* rewards in a medical practice are recognition, celebration, and culture. Recognition can be public praise, personal notice of appreciation, recognition ceremonies, certificates of achievement, and invitations to meaningful events. Celebration can encompass social events, parties, entertainment, practice anniversaries, seasonal events, and birthdays. Creating a positive and energizing culture can be done by encouraging everyone's participation, asking for opinions and recommendations from individuals, developing internal experts, identifying expected behaviors, eliminating *sacred cows* (ie, a person who is often unreasonably immune from criticism or opposition), and recognizing all staff as professionals in their roles.

The way administrators treat their employees can do more to motivate employees than mere wages. Although money is important to a certain extent, it is not the only motivator (or even the most successful one) in most cases.

EFFECTIVE COMMUNICATION

Communication can be improved within the practice by holding staff meetings and actively listening to employees when concerns arise.

Staff Meetings

Staff meetings save the practice time by:

- Reducing interruptions during the workday to answer questions
- Eliminating task repetitions because someone did not know about a recent change
- Lessening the interchange necessary to make a decision

Staff meetings increase productivity in the practice by:

- Clarifying *who* is going to do *what* duties *when*
- Answering specific questions that staff members have about their duties
- Reducing incidences of crisis management

Staff meetings generate better decisions for the practice by:

- Deriving input from staff members who provide different views
- Setting aside a structured time for making decisions through analysis and contemplation

Regular staff meetings are the best vehicles for effective communications. Encourage the team to share ideas for improvement, cost containment, and patient relations. During these meetings, the physician or practice administrator should share details about the practice, talk about the changing health care environment, and explore ideas about how the practice should prepare for these transformations.

Discuss changes in Clinical Laboratory Improvement Act (CLIA), Occupational Safety and Health Administration (OSHA), and Medicare guidelines at these meetings. Even if the government programs do not directly affect the office staff, employees should know the guidelines and how they affect the practice.

Some tips for having an effective staff meeting are:

- Have an agenda and stick to it
- Limit meetings to one hour
- Encourage the physicians to attend

■ Make meetings mandatory

■ Encourage everyone to speak

■ Avoid using staff meetings for disciplinary actions or reprimands

■ Keep the meetings positive and upbeat (no griping allowed)

■ Meet each week; biweekly meetings are acceptable

■ Let each employee be responsible for planning at least one meeting a year (The employee in charge should request input from the rest of the staff to plan the agenda.)

■ Have at least two meetings a year about "fun" issues (An example of an upbeat meeting is to have all share something positive that is going on in their personal lives. This is a good time for each employee to explore a personal or professional goal and solicit everyone's support and help. The physicians should attend these meetings, too, to learn more about their staff.)

During staff meetings, the practice administrator should explain the costs involved in the operation of the practice. Most staff members see only the revenue side of the business and have no perception of how much revenue is spent on overhead. Efficient office procedures control overhead. Therefore, it is important to seek ideas on cost containment and reduction from employees.

Staff meetings provide an ideal time to discuss ways to improve patient relations. Patient relations can be focused on the *Golden Rule*: "Do unto others as you would have them do unto you." In other words, treat patients with respect.

If a problem or issue is introduced in the meeting, use the following format for getting to a resolution. Remember that people will become disenchanted with meetings if problems are never fixed. The following six problem-solving steps can increase the practice's success rate on finding a solution:

■ **Step 1:** Define the problem in the clearest terms. Make sure the issue to be addressed is actually identified.

■ **Step 2:** List the causes of the problem.

■ **Step 3:** List and discuss possible solutions to the problem.

■ **Step 4:** Decide on the best solution.

■ **Step 5:** List all individuals who are involved with and/or affected by the proposed solution. Are they involved in the process?

■ **Step 6:** Try the solution for 30 days and then reopen the issue for discussion.

Active Listening

Unlike hearing, listening does not automatically happen; it is an intellectual and emotional process. Usually a listener's feelings, composed of prior knowledge and experiences with the speaker, interfere with the intellectual portion of listening that analyzes and understands what is being said.

Effective listening is hard work. The average listener understands and retains about 50% of a conversation. The percentage drops to

25% within 48 hours. Misconceptions of what is being said are a consequence of poor listening. This results in the poor listener offering the speaker faulty or inappropriate advice on resolving a perceived problem. The poor listener may even address a totally different problem from the one communicated. Often, such communication leaves the speaker feeling that the listener either does not care or does not know anything about the problem.

Following are typical complaints from employees about an administrator's listening skills:

- He does all the talking; I go in with a problem and never get a chance to open my mouth.
- She interrupts me when I talk.
- He never looks at me when I talk. I'm not sure he's listening.
- She makes me feel as though I'm wasting her time.
- Her facial expressions and body language keep me guessing about whether she is listening to me.
- He stays on the surface of the conversation or problem.

Listeners fall into four categories:

1. **Nonlistener.**   Fakes attention while thinking about unrelated matters. Too busy preparing response to listen to what is being said. Rarely interested in what anyone else has to say. Must always have the last word.

2. **Marginal listener.**   Hears the sounds and words, but does not really listen. This person is a superficial listener. Stays on the surface of the problem; never risks searching deeper. Postpones problems into the future. Easily distracted by own thinking and environment. The marginal listener frequently gives the speaker the impression that they are being listened to and understood. The speaker goes away thinking that everything is resolved, only to be even more devastated when the problem continues because the listener failed to take action.

3. **Valuative listener.**   Actively tries to hear what the speaker is saying, but is not making an effort to understand the speaker's intent. More concerned with content than feelings of the speaker. Remains emotionally detached. Disregards the speaker's vocal intonation, body language, and facial expressions. Typically great in semantics, facts, and statistics while poor in sensitivity, empathy, and understanding.

4. **Active listener.**   Attempts to see things from the speaker's point of view. Listens for the content, intent, and feeling of the message. Nonverbally communicates to the speaker that he or she is truly listening and is interested in hearing what the speaker wants to say. Tries to get a deeper understanding of the other person. Listens not only to what is said and how it is said, but also to what is not being said. Uses questions to encourage speaker to extend the conversation and clarify the message. Probes areas that need to be developed further in order to get a better picture of what the speaker is trying to communicate.

The following are stimulators that will help anyone become an *active listener*:

- It is impossible to listen and talk at the same time. The only interruption a speaker likes is applause.
- Listen for the speaker's main ideas. Ask, "What is the speaker's message?"
- Fight off distractions. Resist the tendency to listen for quirks in delivery.
- Try not to get angry. Emotions of any kind hinder the listening process.
- Do not trust important data to memory. Take brief notes.
- Let others tell their story first. By doing so, more information will be available upon which to base a response.
- Empathize with the speaker. Make an effort to see the speaker's point of view.
- Paraphrase the speaker's ideas and concepts and repeat them back to demonstrate understanding.

The traits of an *active listener* can be summarized with three easy-to-remember actions: *sensing*, *attending*, and *responding*.

- *Sensing* is the ability to recognize and appreciate the silent messages that the speaker is sending.
- *Attending* is the verbal, vocal, and visual messages that the active listener sends to the speaker indicating attentiveness, receptiveness, and acknowledgment of the speaker.
- *Responding* occurs when the listener stimulates the speaker to provide more details, makes the speaker feel understood, and encourages the speaker to reflect upon the problem or concern to develop a better understanding of the situation.

There is power in listening. When listening to others, genuinely listen. They will provide the best approach for meeting their needs. People work hardest at meeting their own needs. Therefore, structure their duties so they may satisfy their personal and professional goals by accomplishing the goals of the practice. In an efficient practice, the needs of the staff and the practice will be aligned.

BUSINESS TALK

According to Larry King,[1] anyone can talk anywhere at anytime by using the following basic principles:

1. The same basic principles apply in business talk as in social conversation. Be direct and open, and be a good listener if you want to be a good talker.
2. If you are talking within your own industry or profession, you can assume the people you are talking to know the technical terms you are using, but you still have to make yourself clear. And if you are talking to people outside your own field, you

have to assume just the opposite—that your audience or other meeting participants do not know your technical terms, so you have to speak in lay language.

3. Time is money. Do not waste the time of the people to which you are talking.

Know what you are talking about, and whether it is a chat in a coworker's office or a full-dress meeting, be prepared.

TIME MANAGEMENT

The first step to effective time management is to realize that we can never effectively manage *time*. We can only effectively manage ourselves.

Many practice administrators use some type of time management techniques advertised or recommended by a friend or coworker. Unfortunately, none of these completely resolve time management problems. Only two factors are important for learning about time management:

- Realizing that one person cannot do it all
- Organizing and executing around priorities

We tend to believe we have accomplished something or had a productive day if we can check off several things on our "to do" list. Yet, we may not have accomplished one thing that improves the three critical areas of the practice:

- Patient care
- Revenue enhancement
- Cost containment

Most of us suffer from an *urgency addiction*. There is a good chance that urgency is a fundamental operational pattern for many. Some of us are so used to the adrenaline rush of handling crises that we are dependent on it for energy and a sense of worth and accomplishment. While it may be stressful, it makes us feel validated and useful.

For some, the mind-set may be, "Whenever there is trouble, we ride into town with our six-shooter, gun the varmint down, and valiantly ride off into the sunset." Our instant results bring instant gratification. Everywhere we turn, urgency addiction is reinforced in our lives and culture.

To be effective time administrators, we must concentrate on what is *important* instead of what is *urgent*. Learning to concentrate on the important reduces our crisis mode and our urgency addiction. The important eventually becomes the urgent. The strategy is to act on the *important* before it becomes the *urgent*.

Figure 5-2 illustrates four types of issues:

- Urgent and important
- Urgent, but not important
- Important, but not urgent
- Not important, not urgent

FIGURE 5-2

What Kind of Issue Is It?

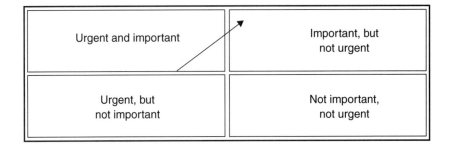

Many managers spend their time focusing on issues in the lower left corner. To become a more successful manager, leaders should shift their focus to those issues that occupy the square in the upper right-hand corner.

Important factors fall under seven key activities:

- Improving communication with people
- Better preparation
- Better planning and organization
- Taking better care of oneself
- Seizing new opportunities
- Personal development
- Empowerment

There are two rules that can assist practice managers to better manage their time. They are: delegate, and organize/prioritize.

Rule #1: Delegate

Many practice managers (usually because of a misplaced sense of responsibility) want to control everything. This unrealistic outlook brings trouble in the long run. If this tends to be the case, this manager may burn brightly for a few months or even years, but will eventually burn out and productivity will cease.

Delegation is the most effective time management tool. *Do not be afraid to delegate responsibility to others for fear that it threatens job security.* Managers of employees who perform well, typically get recognition as a result of their employees' efforts. The true responsibility of a leader is to teach others and allow them to learn new skills. As a manager, it is very rewarding to train and encourage others to improve their skills and level of efficiency and watch them succeed.

The rules of successful delegation are simple:

- Give specific instructions for the job to be done—written is best.
- Monitor their progress without checking up on them.
- Set definite time lines for accomplishments and completion of tasks.
- Consistently give encouragement.

Rule #2: Organize and Prioritize

Time management is critical. There are two very important types of time management of which every practice manager must be aware in order to more smoothly operate the practice. They are personal time management and employee time management.

Personal Time Management

Review your own schedule and assure yourself that you are working on the *important* issues—not just the *urgent* ones. Take a notepad and begin listing all the items on the "to do" list. Include professional and personal goals. Add to the list as items come to mind. Bear in mind that:

- Planning requires more than writing a daily "to do" list. First, a "to do" list limits visions. Daily planning often misses important issues that can only be seen from a broader perspective. By looking at long-term goals for the next 5 years, continual work on the important issues will allow managers to focus on the present and keep crisis management in check. Plan every month at least 30 days in advance; 90 days is better. Start this plan by writing down all continuing functions. Enter on a calendar periodic activities that routinely take place on a specific day each month, such as sending out statements, paying bills, making payroll, conducting performance appraisals, and making collections calls.

- Look at the practice's "to do" list and plan to complete at least one task each month. Plan it. Be selfish. Be proactive, not allowing others to interrupt or control the time set aside for this activity. Take responsibility for what has been accomplished.

- Next, set up the coming week. Prioritize what is important.

- Finally, make a "to do" list for the coming day.

- Write everything down. Carry a small notebook everywhere. Make notes or reminders so nothing is forgotten. Write down all ideas and thoughts.

- Group all work according to type. For example, increase productivity by setting aside specific times for certain tasks, such as returning calls, reviewing the mail, and so forth. Keep all the information or paperwork for each project in a pocket folder. Work on one project at a time in the order of its priority. Allow one or two hours per project; then go on to the next one.

- Carry a portable tape recorder in the car for long commutes. Use this time for thinking and planning. When an idea or thought comes to mind, record it on the tape recorder.

- Use voice mail as a reminder tool. Record personal messages about important meetings or deadlines.

- Allow time for reading and education. Be informed about the changing health care industry. Read all the managed care contracts. Learn about capitation and how to calculate capitation rates. Read about various integration models and the changes in reimbursement patterns.

- Always strive to improve personal skills and increase talents.

- Avoid taking work home. If need be, come in early or stay late. Personal time is for home and family. It benefits no one if personal time is used for work.

- If work is everything, be the first one in the office in the morning and the last one to leave in the evening.

- Set goals. Write them down on 3" × 5" cards and put them in a prominent place, such as on the mirror, the desk, or in the car. If you believe you can do something, you can. Keep a positive attitude about reaching goals.

- Strive for patience.

- At the beginning of each day, focus on two or three primary goals.

- Set a time limit on activities. Use a timer.

- Let the staff members know when they can speak with you and when you wish not to be disturbed.

- Use the "TRAF" method for handling the mail. Look at each piece of mail and decide immediately if you will:

  - *Toss* it in the trash.
  - *Refer* or delegate it to someone else along with the proper instructions.
  - *Act* on it yourself. Do the job immediately if it can be completed in 10 minutes or less.
  - *File* it immediately in your own files, or put it in a desktop tray marked "to be filed." Assign filing responsibilities to a staff member. Filing should be done daily.

- Ask, "What is the best use of my time right now?"

Employee Time Management

Just as was done with the personal schedule, review all employees' schedules to assure efficiency. The following tips will help keep the office running smoothly:

- Have a *stand up* meeting every morning for 10 minutes. Include the physicians, if possible.

- Review the schedule for any special orders or circumstances.

- Give instructions to the staff for jobs that need to be done.

- Discuss with the physicians any calls they may have received at home.

- Get information from the physician that is required for accurate billing of services, diagnoses, or procedures done in the emergency department, hospital, or nursing home.

- Develop a *Practice Policies and Procedures Manual* that defines every job function. Have all employees contribute to the manual by providing an outline of their tasks and functions and how they are handled. Written policies and procedures are a great time-saver, excellent orientation and training resource, and a fundamental part of risk management.

- Encourage all employees to use a daily "to do" list. Help them develop daily and weekly goals. Use the annual performance appraisal for helping employees set personal and professional goals for the coming year. Do not allow them to set goals and then forget about them. Rather, interface with the employees about their goals throughout the year. Offer encouragement and praise, and help, only upon request.

IMPLEMENTING CHANGE

To orchestrate any change, it is important to understand the three basic phases: (1) formative, (2) normative, and (3) integrative.

Phase 1: Formative

Phase 1, the *formative phase*, is the time the concept of change comes into being. There is a search for something new and a strong sense of mission. There is also a lot of tension and uncertainty during this phase, with questions such as, "Are we doing the right thing?" "Is this really going to work?" and "Why can't the rest of them see what a great concept this is?" This is the phase where things happen.

For the most part, change is beyond the control of the line staff, so it is important to consider what effect the change will have on them. Their actions and behavior will be key to successful implementation of the change.

The readiness of the organization to accept change must also be assessed. Although change is always unnerving, some organizations are better equipped to cope with transition than others. The culture of the organization will affect the openness to change. If trust has been established and there is open communication and a team spirit, change will be less disruptive than if morale is low and discontent and suspiciousness are present.

Many organizations find that the creation of a transition team helps people at all levels of the organization to come to grips with change. To form the transitional team, get input from a cross-functional team of individuals. Select key individuals for the team. For example, if the billing and reimbursement processes are to be revised, a billing clerk, a patient account representative, a front desk staff member, and a volunteer should be participants on the transitional team.

During the implementation period, provide proactive troubleshooting. This can include writing and distributing weekly updates, listening to staff members when they say something may not work and asking them to find another solution, and using e-mail or another fast way to get the word out quickly to as many people as possible.

Phase 2: Normative

The second phase — the attempt to return to normalcy — may be either like opening a new office and rebuilding from the ground up or very low key. Probably the most overlooked feature of the change process is training staff members. Just because new protocols and job descriptions are in writing does not mean that staff members fully understand their new roles. Comprehensive training is critical to the success of any change. For example, in addition to providing training on a new computer system, it is advisable to offer an intensive overview of new protocols and job descriptions and to start out on the right foot by setting up some dry runs of the new procedures.

Rewards are also important. The emotional toll on employees should not go unnoticed. Group pizza parties or picnics, gift certificates to movies or video stores, or invitations to sporting events may crystallize the group into the new culture that is sought.

Phase 3: Integrative

Although most people responsible for initiating change realize that it will take time before the office is back to normal, that time often takes longer than originally anticipated.

To make the change less painful:

- Ensure that all physicians are fully committed. Physicians who are not committed to a change can be destructive to the process.
- Clearly define the change vision. For example, "What will this new process look like when it is finished?" "Are the steps written down on paper?" and "Are processes or changes graphed and charted so that staff members and physicians can visualize them?"
- Set objectives for 90 days, 6 months, and 1 year from now.
- Ensure that the nonphysician leaders understand the goal and can empower and lead the staff members through the process.
- Hold regular staff meetings to determine what worked, what did not, and how to make improvements.
- Assign a physician manager to each area that is being reengineered.
- Budget for change. Staff members are going to incur overtime and new equipment will need to be purchased. Prepare in advance for these expenses.
- Train. Train. Train. No amount of training will be excessive—ever.

SUMMARY

Management skills can be honed and finely tuned with knowledge and understanding of teamwork, communication, and time management — but not without effort and planning. Persuading staff members toward change is the ongoing challenge for the accomplished practice manager.

ENDNOTES

1. King, L. *How to Talk to Anyone, Anytime, Anywhere: The Secrets of Good Communications.* New York: Three Rivers Press; 1994, 107–108.

RESOURCES

Murphy, EC. *The Quality Connection.* Amherst, NY:E.C. Murphy, Ltd.; 1990, 7–17.

chapter 6

Employment Law

Employment laws have changed the ways employers treat their workers. The following are a number of laws that have been passed in the last few decades that affect the employee/employer relationship.

STATUTES OVERVIEW—CIVIL AND OTHER RIGHTS

The practice manager should have a working knowledge and a broad reference of all aspects of employment relations and the statutes that form the basis of all employment decisions. Following is a brief overview of laws that govern the medical practice. Extended information is provided on selected statutes thought to be of extreme risk and not easily understood.

The Civil Rights Act of 1964, Title VII

- Prohibits employment discrimination because of race, color, religion, sex, or national origin
- Created the Equal Employment Opportunity Commission (EEOC) to enforce the act
- Applies to employers with 15 or more employees

More information on this legislation is addressed later in this chapter under the section on sexual harassment.

Equal Pay Act of 1963

- Amendment to Fair Labor Standards Act of 1938
- Prohibits wage differential for men and women for jobs that require equal skills, effort, and responsibility when performed under similar working conditions

Age Discrimination in Employment Act of 1967 (ADEA)

- Prohibits discrimination against persons age 40 and older
- Abolishes mandatory retirement at age 65
- Applies to employers with 20 or more employees

Immigration Reform and Control Act

- Prohibits employers from discriminating in employment on the basis of citizenship or nation origin
- Requires employers to verify the identity and employment authorization of all employees
- Applies to employers with as few as four employees

Pregnancy Discrimination Act of 1978

- An amendment to Title VII of the Civil Rights Act, prohibits discrimination on the basis of pregnancy, childbirth, or related medical condition
- Applies to all terms and conditions of employment, including hiring, firing, promotion, leave, and benefits

Consolidated Omnibus Budget Reconciliation Act of 1985 (COBRA)

- Applies to employers of 20 or more employees
- This federal law requires employers to offer employees and their dependents certain health insurance continuation rights if the employee is terminated, laid off, or has his or her hours reduced so that they no longer meet the eligibility requirements for health insurance coverage

If any of those events occur, the employee or dependents can choose to continue health care coverage for 18 months at the employer's group premium rate (plus 2% for administrative costs). Only employees who are terminated due to gross misconduct (eg, behavior that amounts to a crime) can be denied these health insurance continuation rights.

Certain other events, such as an employee's death, divorce, or legal separation, trigger health insurance continuation rights on the part of the employee's dependents for up to 36 months.

If an employer fails to comply with COBRA requirements, the employer may lose its income tax deduction for the expenses for its group health plan, among other sanctions. The practice manager's responsibility is to send any eligible, terminated employee a letter notifying them of their COBRA benefits.

Americans with Disabilities Act of 1990 (ADA)

- The ADA protects persons with disabilities from discrimination in employment, public services, public accommodations, and telecommunications
- Applies to employers with 15 or more employees

Family Medical Leave Act of 1993

- Allows for 12 weeks of unpaid leave for qualified employees with no loss of benefit for the following reasons:

- The birth, adoption, or foster care placement of a child
- To care for a child, spouse, or parent who has a serious health condition requiring personal care
- A serious health condition that causes the employee to be unable to perform the essential functions of the job

■ Affects employers with 50 or more employees within a 75-mile radius

Fair Labor Standards Act of 1938 (FLSA)

■ Establishes minimum wage and overtime pay standards
■ Regulates child labor

The FLSA requires employers to keep records on wages and hours worked. It is essential that the practice knows and can prove the number of hours an employee works each week. Employee compensation should be on record, supported by time cards. The maintenance of this type of documentation facilitates accurate payment for overtime services and adheres to wage and hour laws.

The Department of Labor does not require a special format for wage records as long as they are easily ascertainable. Wage records of each employee should include:

■ Full name as used in Social Security records
■ Social Security number, employee number, or symbol, as used in payroll records
■ Home address, including zip code
■ Date of birth, if under the age of 19
■ Sex
■ Position
■ Time of the day and the day of the week when the employee's work begins
■ Regular hourly rate of pay
■ Amount and type of pay for any pay that is not included in the regular rate
■ Hours worked by the employee on each work day, and the total hours for the week
■ Total daily or weekly earnings (not including any premiums paid for overtime)
■ Total payment of overtime for the work week
■ Total wages for the employee for each pay period
■ Date of each payment made to the employee and the pay period covered by the payment
■ Total amount of additions to or deductions from wages for each pay period
■ For each deduction, the employer must show the following:
  - Date
  - Amount
  - Nature of the deduction

Regardless of whether time clocks or time sheets are used, the important point is to maintain records of employees' work hours for a minimum of 3 years.

A work week is defined as 168 hours during seven consecutive 24-hour periods. It may begin on any day of the week. Each work week stands alone. There can be no averaging of two or more work weeks.

Employees must be paid for all hours worked in a work week. In general, hours worked include all time an employee must be on duty, or on the employer's premises, or in any other prescribed place of work. Also included is any additional time the employee is required or permitted to work. Overtime pay must be paid at a rate of at least one and one-half times the regular rate of pay.

When violations are found or reported, the enforcement division of the FLSA is required to carry out an investigation and gather data on wages, hours, and other employment conditions or practices.

Willful violation can carry a fine up to $10,000. The Secretary of Labor may bring suit against the employer on behalf of the employee, or the employee may bring a private lawsuit. The employee is entitled to all back pay due as well as an additional amount equal to the back wages for liquidated damages. A 2-year statute of limitations applies to recovery of back pay.

Keep in mind the following point regarding the FLSA:

■ Employees are entitled to overtime if they work more than 40 hours in a week. This includes working through their lunch— even if it is not a job requirement. Therefore, all overtime should be preapproved.

Overtime pay is not paid for extra hours worked during a week when the employee is out for sick leave or vacation time because the employee was not physically on the job. Overtime is paid for the hours that exceed 40 hours.

OCCUPATIONAL LAWS AND PROBLEMS IN THE WORKPLACE

In addition to laws relating to workers' and civil rights, several other occupational statutes govern the medical practice.

Workers' Compensation Law

The state rather than federal law governs workers' compensation almost entirely. The purpose of the workers' compensation system is to provide a uniform method of compensating employees for on-the-job injuries at a cost that is evenly distributed through insurance or other assessments against employers. Points to remember are:

■ It is the practice's responsibility to request all information provided by each state's Workers' Compensation Board.
■ Post the required information as directed.
■ Update and keep records of claims.

Workers' Compensation Law is often ignored or forgotten by management once the required information has been posted. However, workplace injuries are increasing, and it is important that supervisors know the steps to follow if an employee is injured on the job.

Most states require employers to comply with the Workers' Compensation Law in one of two ways:

■ Purchasing Workers' Compensation Insurance through a qualified carrier or a state insurance fund.

■ Becoming self-insured by a process prescribed under state law.

Employers that fail to purchase insurance or obtain self-insurance approval lose the immunity normally afforded employers under the Workers' Compensation Law. Answering the following questions will provide a guide for steps to be taken in the event of an injury.

■ Have you established a safety policy? A written policy develops employee awareness and expresses to all employees the intent to provide a safe workplace. Establishing a safe working environment can include posted signs, written rules, standard job procedures, personal protective equipment requirements, compliance with equipment codes, and rules for disposal of hazardous waste. Common steps in a safety program include:
  – Remove the hazard, if possible.
  – If the hazard cannot be removed, guard against it.
  – If it cannot be effectively guarded, use personal protective equipment to protect employees from the hazard.
  – Supervise and train employees to work safely and to be aware of the risks.
  – Complete the Employee Safety Orientation Checklist/Injury and Illness Prevention for each employee (see Figure 6-1).

■ Does the practice know the name of the workers' compensation insurance carrier, the claims process, and the benefits involved?

■ Does the practice have First Report of Injury forms, or does it know carrier's procedures (ie, telephone reporting procedures)?

■ Does every manager and supervisor in the practice know how to administer first aid?

■ Do all employees know where to report injuries?

■ Is every accident and injury investigated?

■ Do all employees know who the practice's medical provider is (see *Dual Capacity Doctrine* in the following section of this chapter)?

■ If a state permits the practice to direct an injured employee to a selected provider, do the employees know which providers are preferred? Who the medical provider panel is?

■ Is the practice's workers' compensation policy aimed at getting the employee back to work?

■ Are return-to-work goals stated on every claim that is filed?

FIGURE 6-1

Employee Safety Orientation Checklist

EMPLOYEE SAFETY ORIENTATION CHECKLIST

Injury and Illness Prevention

Employee Name: _____

Title: _____

Is this a new employee?	❏	Yes	❏	No
Is this a new job assignment?	❏	Yes	❏	No

1. Has the employee received instruction with respect ❏ Yes ❏ No
   to general safety and health work practices?
      If yes, when? _____

2. Has the employee received instruction on:

Emergency procedures?	❏	Yes	❏	No
Injury and illness prevention?	❏	Yes	❏	No
Safety discipline policy?	❏	Yes	❏	No
Hazard communication?	❏	Yes	❏	No
Hazardous material identification system?	❏	Yes	❏	No

3. Has the employee received safety training on the hazards ❏ Yes ❏ No
   specific to his/her job assignment?

4. Does the employee have any known illnesses or ailments that ❏ Yes ❏ No
   will hamper him/her in the performance of the job
   assignment?

5. Does the employee understand that he/she is required to ❏ Yes ❏ No
   work safely at all times and is responsible for safety while in
   the facility?

6. Has the employee received a copy of the Safe Work ❏ Yes ❏ No
   Practices and Safety Rules?

_____   _____
                Employee's Signature   Date

_____   _____
                Instructor's Name   Date

■ Are injured employees kept working on the job site whenever possible, even if in a lesser capacity or role?

■ Is the injured person visited on a regular basis to provide support and offer assistance?

■ What should be said and done when visiting an injured employee?

For matters relating to workers' compensation, keep the following tips in mind:

■ The required information must be posted in a place that is accessible and in full view of all employees. The break room is an excellent location. Include a checklist for handling an accident.

■ Know the carrier's procedures for reporting claims.

■ Know each state's requirements for choosing a panel of medical providers.

Dual Capacity Doctrine

The dual capacity doctrine is sometimes used against medical employers that treat their own employees. If an employee is injured by an employer acting in the role of a third-party provider of medical services, the provider may be liable for injuries that result from the medical treatment. Although an accident may occur on the premises of a qualified medical provider, because of exposure to liability risks under the dual capacity doctrine, another provider should render medical care for an on-the-job injury.

Therefore, after the injured employee receives first aid, the employee should receive medical attention from a prearranged provider. A physician should not enter into the dual role of employer and physician to the employee. The practice administrator or the physician should choose a medical provider that he or she would personally consult.

Immediate Response to Injury or Accident

Use the following steps to develop a plan for responding to a workers' compensation injury in the practice.

1. Handling an accident:
   ■ Respond quickly and administer first aid.
   ■ Determine if the injury is covered by workers' compensation.
   ■ Accompany the injured worker to a selected medical provider.
   ■ Report the accident within the practice (ie, to physician or practice manager).
   ■ File an accident report. Report the injury to the Workers' Compensation Insurance Carrier using the First Report of Injury forms, as required by law.
   ■ Notify the family.

2. First day after the injury:
   ■ Follow-up with the employee.
   ■ Conduct an accident investigation. Consider every injury legitimate. (See samples of Accident/Injury Reports in Figures 6-2, 6-3, and 6-4.)

Sample of an Accident/Injury Report for an Employer

ACCIDENT/INJURY REPORT - EMPLOYER

Date of Accident/Injury: _____ / _____ / _____   **Name of Injured Employee:** _____

Job Title: _____   **How Long in this Position?** _____

Were paramedics called?   ❑ Yes   ❑ No

Was employee: ❑ sent to hospital   ❑ clinic   Did employee receive first aid?   ❑ Yes   ❑ No

What was the employee doing when the injury/accident occurred? _____
_____
_____

Was the employee trained to do this work?   ❑ Yes   ❑ No

Has the employee performed this work before?   ❑ Yes   ❑ No   If yes, how often? _____

How recently was employee assigned the task that gave rise to the
accident?   _____

Based on your investigation, how did the accident/injury occur? _____
_____
_____

Have any similar accidents occurred in the last 12 months?   ❑ Yes   ❑ No   If yes, how many? _____

What can be done to prevent a similar incident from occurring in the future? _____
_____
_____

Have any corrective measures been implemented?   ❑ Yes   ❑ No

Specify: _____
_____
_____

Possible Causes of Injury or Illness (check all that apply)

Employer Responsibilities	Employee Responsibilities	Unsafe Equipment or Material	Unsafe Conditions
❑ No instruction given	❑ Haste or short cuts	❑ Inadequate guarding	❑ Poor light
❑ Incomplete instruction	❑ Did not use proper equipment	❑ Defective equipment	❑ Poor ventilation
❑ Lack of enforcement of safe work practices	❑ Did not use safe work practices	❑ Poor design	❑ Congestion
❑ Lack of proper tools or equipment	❑ Horseplay	❑ Other	❑ Improper piling or storing
❑ Equipment in poor condition	❑ Disregard for instruction		❑ Inadequate exits
❑ Lack of safe work practices	❑ Did not pay attention		❑ Obstructed walkways
	❑ Action of another employee		❑ Poor housekeeping
❑ Haste	❑ Physical condition of employee		❑ Other
❑ Other	❑ Other		

This report was prepared by: _____

                                                          Print Name/Title

_____

Signature   Date

FIGURE 6-3

Sample of an Accident/Injury Report for an Employee

ACCIDENT/INJURY REPORT - EMPLOYEE

Note: The purpose of this report is not to assign blame. Rather, we are attempting to find out how the accident/injury occurred so that we can keep it from happening in the future.

Date of Accident/Injury: ____ / ____ / ____ **Name of Injured Employee:** _____

Job Title: _____ **How Long in this Position?** _____

What were you doing when the injury/accident occurred? _____
_____

Have you performed this work before? ❏ Yes ❏ No If yes, how often? _____

Describe in detail how the accident/injury occurred _____
_____

What can be done to prevent a similar incident from occurring in the future? _____
_____
_____

Have any corrective measures been implemented? ❏ Yes ❏ No

Specify: _____
_____
_____

Possible Causes of Injury or Illness (check all that apply)

Employer Responsibilities	**Employee Responsibilities**	**Unsafe Equipment or Material**	**Unsafe Conditions**
❏ No instruction given	❏ Haste or short cuts	❏ Inadequate guarding	❏ Poor light
❏ Incomplete instruction	❏ Did not use proper equipment	❏ Defective equipment	❏ Poor ventilation
❏ Lack of enforcement of safe work practices	❏ Did not use safe work practices	❏ Poor design	❏ Congestion
❏ Lack of proper tools or equipment	❏ Horseplay	❏ Other	❏ Improper piling or storing
❏ Equipment in poor condition	❏ Disregard for instruction		❏ Inadequate exits
❏ Lack of safe work practices	❏ Did not pay attention		❏ Obstructed walkways
❏ Haste	❏ Action of another employee		❏ Poor housekeeping
❏ Other	❏ Physical condition of employee		❏ Other
	❏ Other		

Signature   Date

FIGURE 6-4
Sample of an Accident/Injury Report for a Witness

ACCIDENT/INJURY REPORT - WITNESS

Note: The purpose of this report is not to assign blame. Rather, we are attempting to find out how the accident/injury occurred so that we can keep it from happening in the future.

Date of Accident/Injury: ___/___/___   **Name of Injured Employee:** _____

Injured Employee Job Title: _____

Your Name: _____

Your Job Title: _____ **How Long in this Position?** _____

What was the employee doing when the injury/accident occurred? _____
_____

Have you performed this work before?   ❏ Yes   ❏ No   If yes, how often? _____

Describe in detail how the accident/injury occurred _____
_____

What can be done to prevent a similar incident from occurring in the future? _____
_____
_____

Have any corrective measures been implemented?   ❏ Yes   ❏ No

Specify: _____
_____
_____

Possible Causes of Injury or Illness (check all that apply)

Employer Responsibilities	Employee Responsibilities	Unsafe Equipment or Material	Unsafe Conditions
❏ No instruction given	❏ Haste or short cuts	❏ Inadequate guarding	❏ Poor light
❏ Incomplete instruction	❏ Did not use proper equipment	❏ Defective equipment	❏ Poor ventilation
❏ Lack of enforcement of safe work practices	❏ Did not use safe work practices	❏ Poor design	❏ Congestion
❏ Lack of proper tools or equipment	❏ Horseplay	❏ Other	❏ Improper piling or storing
❏ Equipment in poor condition	❏ Disregard for instruction		❏ Inadequate exits
❏ Lack of safe work practices	❏ Did not pay attention		❏ Obstructed walkways
❏ Haste	❏ Action of another employee		❏ Poor housekeeping
❏ Other	❏ Physical condition of employee		❏ Other
	❏ Other		

Signature   Date

- Counsel the employee and/or family on claims procedures, available benefits, and the practice's continuing interest in the employee's welfare. (It is important for the administrator to have a working knowledge of workers' compensation procedures and benefits.)

3. Continuing involvement is the key to controlling claims:
   - Typically, it is the employee who is ignored by the employer who seeks an attorney to help get the benefits to which he or she is entitled.
   - Communicate continued concern for the employee's well-being.

4. First week after the injury:
   - Make sure the insurer has contacted the employee about benefits and payment.
   - Talk to the treating physician to learn the diagnosis and treatment plan.
   - Develop a return-to-work plan. Can the employee accept a light duty assignment?
   - Stay in touch with the injured employee.

5. First month after the injury:
   - Calls, letters, and visits reinforce concern.
   - Stay in touch with the treating physician for updates on the employee's condition and any changes in treatment or diagnosis.

Keeping the employee informed about his or her rights under Workers' Compensation Law is extremely important.

OSHA Workplace Requirements

The Occupational Safety and Health Administration (OSHA) was enacted in 1970 to ensure safe and healthful working conditions for employees. OSHA requirements imposed on employers are found in regulations and safety standards that are issued through the Secretary of Labor.

Medical employers have unique concerns for employee health and safety. The practice manager has specific responsibility if an employee is exposed to a bloodborne pathogen or other potentially hazardous material. Employees must be trained to follow the Exposure Incident Protocol (Figure 6-5). An Employee Safety Orientation Checklist/Injury and Illness Prevention must be completed on each employee. This form should be a part of the office's procedure manual. The manager should personally complete or supervise the completion of the Exposure Incident Report (Figure 6-6) if an incident occurs. In addition to the incident report, the manager should also complete or supervise the completion of Post-Exposure Incident Forms (Figures 6-7 and 6-8).

FIGURE 6-5

Exposure Incident Protocol

EXPOSURE INCIDENT PROTOCOL

1. Upon exposure to blood or other potentially infectious material, the employee will wash hands and any other skin surface that my have been exposed and will flush with water mucous membranes that may have been in contact with blood or other potentially infectious materials as soon as feasible after exposure.

2. Following washing/flushing as described above, the employee will report the following incident to Dr _____ or to _____

    _____

3. Dr _____ or _____ will make arrangements for post-exposure evaluation and follow-up with (provider) _____

    _____

4. Dr _____ or _____ will ensure that the provider has given the information listed on the *Post-Exposure Incident Report* and a copy of the OSHA regulations to the health care provider.

5. A copy of the written opinion of the health care provider is obtained within 15 days of the medical evaluation.

6. One copy of the written opinion is given to the employee, and a second copy is filed with the employee medical record.

7. The exposure incident is evaluated and a report of the incident is written by _____

    _____

FIGURE 6-6

Exposure Incident Report

EXPOSURE INCIDENT REPORT

Confidential Employee Medical Record

_____

Employee Name (Please print)   Date of Incident

_____

Social Security Number   Time of Incident

The Incident

What task or procedure was the employee performing at the time of the incident?

_____

How did the incident occur?

_____

_____

What type of body fluid was involved in the incident? _____

The route of exposure was:

Needlestick with contaminated needle to (site) _____

Piercing of skin with contaminated sharp to (site) _____

Splashing/spraying of potentially infectious material to (site) _____

Other (describe) _____

_____

The following remedial action may reduce the likelihood of similar incidents in the future:

_____

_____

This recommendation was instituted on _____ (date)

FIGURE 6-7

Post-Exposure Incident Form—Source

POST-EXPOSURE INCIDENT FORM—SOURCE

Source Individual Consent Form

_____

Patient Name (Please print)   Social Security Number

Informed Consent to Blood Testing

I have been informed that an individual has been exposed to my blood or body fluids. As a result of the exposure, I have been asked to permit my blood to be tested for HIV (known to cause AIDS) and HBV.

(check one)

❏ I hereby give my consent to such testing

❏ I consent to have my blood tested for HBV, but I decline to have my blood tested for HIV at this time. I understand that by choosing this option, a sample of my blood will be kept for 90 days, during which period I may change my mind and have my blood tested for HIV at that time.

My consent is based on the understanding that:

1. My test results will remain confidential and provided only to those who have a need to know in accordance with current federal, state, and local statutes.

2. I have been provided with information concerning HIV and HBV, and understand the contents thereof.

3. I have been given the opportunity to ask questions concerning HIV and HBV testing.

4. I will receive a copy of all test results.

_____

Signature   Date

Employer's Representative

I certify that the above-named individual received copies of the HIV/HBV information sheets and has had the contents thereof fully explained.

_____

Date   Employer's Representative (Please print)

                              _____

                              Title

                              _____

                              Signature

This document will be retained in the exposed employee's medical file.

FIGURE 6-8
Post-Exposure Incident Form—Employee

POST-EXPOSURE INCIDENT FORM—EMPLOYEE

Exposed Employee Consent Form

_____

Employee Name (Please print)   Social Security Number

Employee Consent to Blood Testing

As a result of my exposure to blood or other potentially infectious material, it is recommended that I have my blood tested for HIV (known to cause AIDS) and HBV.

(check one)

❑ I hereby give my consent to such testing.

❑ I consent to have my blood tested for HBV, but I decline to have my blood tested for HIV at this time. I understand that by choosing this option, a sample of my blood will be kept for 90 days, during which period I may change my mind and have my blood tested for HIV at that time.

My consent is based on the understanding that:

1. My test results will remain confidential and provided only to those who have a need to know in accordance with current federal, state, and local statutes.

2. I will be provided with counseling whether the tests are negative or positive.

3. I will be provided with information concerning HIV and HBV, and understand the contents thereof.

4. I will be given the opportunity to ask questions concerning HIV and HBV testing.

5. I have received risk behavior guidelines concerning HIV.

6. I will receive a copy of all test results.

_____

Signature   Date

Employer's Representative

I certify that the above-named individual received copies of the HIV/HBV information sheets and has had the contents thereof fully explained.

_____

Date   Employer's Representative (Please print)

_____

                                     Title

_____

                                     Signature

This document will be retained in the exposed employee's medical file.

Sexual Harassment under Title VII

Sexual harassment includes unwelcome sexual advances, requests for sexual favors, and other verbal or physical conduct of a sexual nature. The guidelines state that such conduct violates Title VII of the Civil Rights Act of 1964 when:

- Submission to such conduct is made a term or condition of an individual's employment.
- Submission to or rejection of such conduct is used as the basis for employment decisions affecting an individual (eg, denial of a pay increase, promotion, transfer, leave of absence, imposing disciplinary action, promising to withhold disciplinary action).
- Such conduct interferes with performance or creates an offensive environment.

Title VII places responsibility on the employer for the conduct of others:

- **Supervisors.**   The employer is liable for the acts of its officers, agents, and supervisors with respect to sexual harassment, regardless of whether the employer knew or should have known about the unlawful conduct.
- **Actions of nonsupervisory employees.**   The employer is responsible for the acts of sexual harassment occurring between fellow employees where the employer, its agent, or supervisors knew or should have known about the unlawful conduct, unless the employer can show that it took "immediate and appropriate corrective action." The guidelines do not define what is meant by "immediate and appropriate corrective action."
- **Actions of nonemployees.**   The employer is also liable for the actions of nonemployees (eg, patients, outside sales representatives, contractors, delivery personnel) with respect to sexual harassment in the workplace when the employer knew or should have known of the conduct and failed to take immediate and appropriate corrective action.

The employer is responsible for taking preventive actions to avoid sexual harassment. Suggested actions are:

- Raising the subject of sexual harassment with the workforce and expressing strong disapproval
- Developing appropriate sanctions and penalties when unlawful conduct is committed
- Advising employees of their right to raise and how to raise sexual harassment claims under Title VII
- Developing methods to sensitize all concerned

Sexual harassment is defined broadly by Title VII guidelines. The range of conduct that may be viewed as unlawful may vary widely with the sensitivity of the individual.

Responsive actions of employers are:

- Adopt and publicize to all employees a written policy statement that prohibits sexual harassment in the workplace
- Adopt an in-house complaint resolution procedure
- Fully and promptly investigate sexual harassment complaints
- Explain the policies to staff members

The liability imposed on employers for sexual harassment suggests that special efforts must be exerted to minimize the legal risk. Title VII prohibits an employer from retaliating against an employee for the employee's opposition to an unlawful employment practice or for asserting any rights granted under the Civil Rights Act.

Generally, employees do not fully understand the far-reaching ramifications of sexual harassment. Conduct an in-service training session for all employees to explain the practice's in-house complaint and resolution procedures. Answer any concerns employees may have.

Americans with Disabilities Act (ADA)

The ADA protects persons with disabilities from discrimination in employment, public services, public accommodations, and telecommunications. The employment provisions of the ADA became effective July 26, 1992. Employers with 15 or more employees are affected by this act as of July 26, 1994.

Anti-Discrimination Provisions
The ADA law prohibits covered employers from discrimination against a "qualified individual with a disability." With respect to an individual, a *disability* means: "A physical or mental impairment that substantially limits one or more of the major life activities of such individual. . . ." A *physical or mental impairment* means any physiological disorder or condition, cosmetic disfigurement, or anatomical loss affecting most body systems, and mental or psychological disorders, such as mental illness, learning disabilities, mental retardation, and so forth. It includes HIV infection and AIDS.

A person who has been successfully rehabilitated and who no longer uses illegal drugs or abuses alcohol is considered a person with a disability and thus is protected by the ADA. (Current use of alcohol that prevents an individual from performing his/her duties is not protected.)

A *qualified individual with a disability* is defined as "an individual with a disability who, with or without reasonable accommodation, can perform the essential functions of the employment position that such individual holds or desires." If an employer has prepared a written job description before advertising or interviewing applicants for the job, this job description will be considered evidence of the essential functions of the job. If, for example, a person in a wheelchair applies for a switchboard operator position, the essential function being to answer the telephone, his or her disability has no relevance in assessing the individual's qualifications for that job. The same is not true if the person is deaf and applies for that position.

Reasonable Accommodation

The ADA requires an employer to make *reasonable accommodation* for an individual's disability. However, the employer need not incur *undue hardship*. Reasonable accommodation may include:

- Making existing facilities readily accessible to and usable by persons with disabilities
- Job restructuring
- Part-time or modified work schedules
- Reassignment to a vacant position
- Acquisition or modification of equipment or devices
- Appropriate adjustment or modifications of examinations, training materials, or policies
- The provision of qualified readers or interpreters
- Other similar accommodations

Whether an action is a *reasonable accommodation* or an *undue hardship* will depend on the particular circumstances. Factors that will be considered are:

- The overall financial resources of the employer
- The overall size of the business with respect to the number of employees and the number, type, and location of its facilities
- The type of operation maintained, including the composition, structure, and functions of the entire workforce
- The nature and cost of the accommodations that are needed

While it is clear that more is required than a minimal effort or expenditure, the type of effort or expenditure will vary from case to case. Key points worth noting about the ADA are as follows:

- In a leased space, both the lessee and the lessor are responsible for making the premises accessible to the people with disabilities.
- An example of *reasonable accommodation* is the installation of a bell or buzzer at the door of the building to alert someone that a person with a disability needs help. An *undue hardship* is installing an elevator in a two-story building where only stairs exist.

The ADA provides that an employer may not conduct medical examinations or make medical inquiries of a job applicant or employee about whether such applicant or employee is an individual with a disability or about the nature or severity of the disability unless the examination or inquiry is job-related and justified by business necessity.

Enforcement

The EEOC enforces the ADA in the same manner as it enforces Title VII of the Civil Rights Act of 1964. The same remedies that apply to Title VII apply to the ADA. Currently those remedies include reinstatement, back pay, and compensatory and punitive damages.

Age Discrimination in Employment Act of 1967 (ADEA)

It is unlawful for an employer to discipline or discharge an employee who is more than 40 years old because of the employee's age. The ADEA does not regulate job-related discipline. The purpose of the law is to eliminate discrimination in employment based simply on the fact that an employee (age 40 and more) is getting older. If an employee is no longer able to meet uniformly applied production standards, discipline or discharge is not unlawful.

■ **Enforcement.** Enforcement of the ADEA is the responsibility of the EEOC. Suits to enforce the law may be brought either by the individual employee or by the government and may result in back pay and reinstatement. An employer's willful violation of the Act could result in additional damages in an amount equal to the back pay, a fine of not more than $10,000, and imprisonment for up to 6 months.

FEDERAL RECORD KEEPING REQUIREMENTS

Following is a list of the types of records and retention periods that federal laws require employer's to keep.

Applications for Employment
■ Required by ADEA and Title VII, 1964 Civil Rights Act
■ One year

Advertisements to Hire Employees
■ Required by ADEA
■ One year

Certificates of Age
■ Required by FLSA
■ Duration of employment of individuals under the age of 18

Discrimination Complaint Records and Actions
■ Required by Title VII, the ADEA, Rehabilitation Act, and Vietnam Era Veterans' Readjustment Assistance Act
■ Until final disposition

ERISA Plan Disclosure; Annual Summaries, and Annual Reports
■ Required by ERISA
■ Six years after filing data

Employment Contracts
■ Required by FLSA
■ Three years

Employment History: Promotions, Demotions, Transfers, Layoffs, Terminations, Pay Rate, and Training
- Required by Title VII, Civil Rights Act of 1964, and ADEA
- One year

Hiring Requests to Employment Agencies
- Required by Title VII, Civil Rights Act of 1964, and the ADEA
- One year

Immigration Documentation
- Required by Immigration Reform and Control Act (Form I-9)
- Three years from date of hire or 1 year from date of termination, whichever is later

Injury Summary
- Required by OSHA Form 101
- Three years
- First aid records for injuries covering lost work time required for 5 years

Medical Records
- Required by OSHA for employees with certain occupational exposures (including exposure to bloodborne pathogens)
- Duration of employment, plus 30 years

Order, Shipping, Billing, and Payment Records
- Required by FLSA
- Three years

Payroll Records
- Required by FLSA, Child Labor Law, Equal Pay Act, Title VII, and ADEA
- Three years

Physical Examination Results
- Required by Title VII and ADEA
- One year

Sale and Purchase Agreements
- Required by FLSA
- Three years

Tests: Employer-Administered Aptitude or Other Employment Tests
- Required by Title VII and ADEA
- One year

Training Records
- Required by OSHA's Bloodborne Pathogens Standard
- Three years

Wage Records: Time Cards, Rate Tables, Work Schedules, etc.
- Required by FLSA and Equal Pay Act
- Two years

Wages Paid, including Additions to or Deductions from Wages Paid
- Required by FLSA
- Three years

Table 6-1 is a compilation of the information on retention of records. The safest course is to retain all records for 4 to 6 years. Some states dictate that individual personnel files for terminated employees be kept for a minimum of 3 years.

FEDERAL REGULATIONS AND REQUIREMENTS

Table 6-2 is a general list of laws, acts, statutes, and regulations and the number of employees an employer must have to be required to comply. State's statutes vary. Check with your state for specific laws and compliance requirements.

TABLE 6-1

Record Retention Table

Record	Minimum Amount of Time to Retain
Time Cards, Time Sheets, Overtime, etc.	2 years required under FLSA, 29 CFR
Employee Earnings Statements	2 years under FLSA
Payroll Records	3 years under FLSA, ADEA, and EPA
Personnel Files	1 to as many as 6 years after termination
I-9 (Immigration) Form	3 years or 1 year after termination
Injury Records	5 years under OSHA and Workers' Comp.
EEO-1 Reports	Forever under 1964 & 1991 Civil Rights Acts
Summary Plan Descriptions Under ERISA	6 years

TABLE 6-2

General Regulations and Requirements

No. of Employees	Law, Act, Statute, or Regulation + Requirement
100+	Affirmative Action Plan (if a government subcontractor)
50+	Filing an EEO-1 Report (Executive Order 11246)
50+	Rehabilitation Act of 1973 (see ADA)
50+	1993 Federal Family Medical Leave Act
25+	Drug Free Workplace Act
20+	COBRA (in California and New Jersey two or more employees)
15+	Civil Rights Acts of 1964 and 1991
15+	Americans with Disabilities Act (ADA)
15+	Federal Pregnancy Discrimination Act
4+	Immigration Reform and Control Act
1+	Federal Fair Labor Standards Act (FLSA)

POSTING REQUIREMENTS

Federal and state laws often require employers to post a notice about a particular law. Employee notices are usually provided as posters or permits and should be posted in a conspicuous place easily accessible to all employees (ie, the break room).

Listed below are the posters that employers are required to display under federal law. Not all are required of every employer. Refer to the specifications previously listed in this chapter to see if the practice qualifies.

■ Age Discrimination, Disability Discrimination, Equal Employment
  – Poster titled "Equal Employment Opportunity is the Law"
  – Available from EEOC offices

■ Child Labor, Minimum Wage, and Overtime
  – Wage-hour poster 1088 (Federal Minimum Wage)
  – Available from the US Department of Labor

■ Family and Medical Leave
  – Poster required by Family and Medical Leave Act of 1993
  – Available from the US Department of Labor

■ Polygraph Testing
  – Wage-hour poster 1462 (Employee Polygraph Protection Act)
  – Available from the US Department of Labor

■ Safety
  – OSHA poster 2203 (Job Safety & Health Protection)
  – Available from the US Department of Labor
  – OSHA also requires posting an annual summary of job injuries (OSHA Form 200)

The posters may be obtained from the government agency charged with enforcing a particular law. Most agencies have developed a single poster that satisfies the requirements of several different laws administered by that agency. There are also private companies that publish posters that employers are required to have.

Contact the following agencies to obtain these posters:

Equal Employment Opportunity Poster Office
2401 E Street NW
Washington, DC 20507

US Department of Labor Posters
200 Constitution Ave. NW, Room S-3502
Washington, DC 20210

EMPLOYMENT CATEGORIES

The administrator should become familiar with the laws governing work hours and wage payments, including minimum wages, overtime, deductions from wages, and child labor. Refer to the section on the FLSA to obtain a working knowledge of this national policy on minimum wages and overtime payments, found earlier in this chapter. A complex law, the FLSA determines whether an employer is subject to federal minimum wage and overtime requirements. Most medical employees are covered. First, ascertain the status of the practice. Then, conclude the exempt or nonexempt status of each employee.

Exempt

The following employment categories have been adapted for application to the medical practice for defining employees who are exempt from overtime pay requirements.

An *Executive Employee* must meet all of the following definitions to be exempt (Practice Managers are typically considered exempt.):

- Primary duty consists of the management of the practice or a customarily recognized department.
- Must supervise at least two full-time employees.
- Must have authority to hire and fire or to recommend those actions.
- Must regularly exercise discretionary powers.
- Must spend no more than 20% of working hours on nonmanagement duties.

An *Administrative Employee* must meet the following definitions to be exempt (Administrative assistants, personnel directors, office managers, and laboratory supervisors are typically considered exempt.):

- Primary duty is to be responsible for office or nonmanual work directly related to management policy or general business operations.
- Must regularly exercise discretion and independent judgment. Must have authority to make important decisions.
- Must assist the executive.
- Must not spend more than 20% of the workweek in nonadministrative duties.

A *Professional Employee* must meet all of the following requirements to be exempt (Physicians, registered nurses, registered or certified medical technologists, physician assistants, speech pathologists, and physical therapists are typically considered exempt.):

- Primary duty must involve work that requires knowledge of an advanced type in a field of science, usually obtained by a prolonged course of specialized instruction and study.
- Must consistently exercise discretion and judgment.
- Must do work that is mainly intellectual and varied.
- Must not spend more than 20% of the workweek on activities not a part of or incident to professional duties.

Nonexempt

Among common positions that typically are considered nonexempt are the following:

- Licensed practical nurses
- Nurse's aides
- Laboratory technicians or assistants
- Clerical workers
- Orderlies
- Food service employees
- Janitorial employees

At-Will Contracts

The most common type of employment agreement in the health care industry is an oral *at-will* agreement. This establishes a relationship in which the employer and employee work at the will of the other. The practice manager must understand this relationship.

- **Concept.**   Just as an employee can resign at any time, so can the employer terminate the employee at any time, for any reason.
- **Exceptions.**   *At will* does not apply to a job in which a contract is in effect stating a specific period of employment. The right of the employer to apply the *at-will* doctrine does not override the restrictions placed on the employer, such as the discriminations defined in Title VII of the 1964 Civil Rights Act.

By using the term *at will* versus *just cause*, an employee serves at the discretion of the medical practice and therefore may be dismissed with or without cause. Utilization of the term *just cause* sets a prerequisite that justifiable cause must be shown in order to discharge an employee.

The practice's employee handbook should indicate that employees of the practice are employees *at will*.

SUMMARY

The practice manager must have a working knowledge of a wide range of federal, state, and local employment-discrimination and occupational laws to circumvent problems in the workplace and to minimize the practice's exposure to legal liability.

chapter 7

Patient Satisfaction

How important is patient satisfaction in the medical practice? Consider this. Patients who are more satisfied with their physicians and the practice in general are more likely to:

- Remain with that physician
- Refer others to that practice
- Comply with the physician's orders and requests
- Pay their bill in a timely manner

In addition, patients who are happy with their physician and the office are generally less likely to sue for malpractice or become a whistle-blower because of a compliance issue. Add to that the fact that managed care organizations consider patient satisfaction highly important when determining which providers will be on their provider panel.

PATIENT SATISFACTION

What makes a patient a satisfied patient? When asked, patients rated the following attributes as important to their satisfaction with the office experience as having a physician who is technically competent:

- Attentiveness, good listening skills
- On-time appointment schedule
- Friendly, courteous, and competent staff
- Modern, clean office with ample parking
- Error-free billing
- Prompt callbacks

Attentiveness, Good Listening Skills

It is a human desire to be listened to and understood. That desire is especially prevalent when a person with ailments or medical conditions sees a physician. However, patients often complain that their physician does not listen to them or give them enough time to understand their problems. The failure to listen actually begins when patients first enter a physician's suite and are told to sign in and have a seat. Later they are told to take off their clothes, put on a paper gown, cough, say "Ah," hold out their arm, take medicine, call back in 3 days, and on and on. Rarely does the medical staff stop to listen, even when the patient has a problem with medication, billing, or questions on his or her condition. The questions are probably ones that both the physician or office staff has heard many times prior, and before the question is even completed, someone (either physician or staff member) comes up with the answer.

Therefore the first step in improving a patient's satisfaction is to improve the listening skills of both the physician and the staff members. Communication experts tell us that there are three steps to good communication. They are:

- **Step 1:** The speaker states an idea, thought, question, or fact while the listener listens.
- **Step 2:** The listener acknowledges what they have heard or said either by paraphrasing what they heard or asking questions to clarify what they did not understand.
- **Step 3:** The listener then responds to the speaker.

In the haste to take care of the patient, Step 2, acknowledging and understanding the patient's question, is often omitted. We go directly to Step 3, which is to respond to the patient, often in a form of direct orders. This hurried, often abrupt answer in response to a patient's expressing dissatisfaction is the result of the need to get the unpleasantness out of the way as quickly as possible. However, this rarely convinces the patient that the physician is in control when this is done. By adding Step 2, the physician can make communication more effective and indicate to the patient that he or she has been attentive to the problems. Consider the difference in the following conversations.

Patient: "Is the doctor running late? I've been here for 30 minutes past my appointment time. I have to pick up my daughter from school in an hour."

Staff member: "The doctor had an emergency. He'll be with you shortly, if you will have a seat."

While this conversation may or may not address the problem in the eyes of the staff member, it probably does not address the concern on the part of the patient, which is, "Will I be home in time to pick up my daughter from school?" Consider how much more patient-friendly and attentive conversation is when we use the three-step method.

- **Step 1:** *Patient:* "Is the doctor running late? I've been here for 30 minutes past my appointment time. I have to pick up my daughter from school in an hour."
- **Step 2:** *Staff Member:* "Mrs. Jones, I'm so sorry you're having to wait. And I understand your concern about being able to pick up your daughter on time."
- **Step 3:** *Respond:* "There was an emergency that took longer than we expected. Let me see how much longer it will be so that you aren't late picking up your daughter."

In the second example, the patient no doubt felt like the staff member understood the concern far better than in the first.

Remembering to use the three steps to good communication in all of our patient encounters will let the patient know that he or she is really cared about as an individual.

Other ways for a physician to show he or she is listening is for the physician to sit down in the examination room while discussing a patient's condition, even if it is only for a few moments. The physician should look the patient in the eye rather than at the chart or a computer monitor. For staff members, telling a patient that some notes will be taken on the conversation before beginning to write or looking away at a computer monitor may indicate that the staff member is still actively involved with the listening and is simply trying to record the facts. One way to improve satisfaction is to improve listening skills with the staff. This could be a topic for an office staff meeting where one staff member plays the part of a patient and another staff member plays the part of a staff member.

On-Time Appointment Schedule

Appointment schedules are discussed in detail in Chapter 9 of this book. However, it is important for physicians and their office staff to realize how important on-time appointments are to patient satisfaction. A study conducted on patient wait times[1] showed that when surveyed on their likeliness of returning to a practice:

- 98% of the patients who rated promptness as "excellent" would return
- 90% of patients who rated promptness as "very good" would return
- 83% of patients who rated promptness as "good" would return
- 68% of patients who rated promptness as "poor" would return

This information indicates that a patient's satisfaction with the promptness clearly has an effect on whether the patient returns to that particular practice for medical care.

Patients need to be informed when the physician is going to be late. Physicians who consistently run late and keep their patients waiting may lose patients without even realizing it. Only one patient out of many will actually complain about the wait time. The others will just find other physicians. Therefore, if timeliness is a problem in the office, steps should be taken to improve the appointment schedule. This may require seeing fewer patients, adding a mid-level provider to take care of some of the overload, taking steps to minimize physician interruptions, or performing a time-motion study to identify where the delays occur.

Friendly, Courteous, and Competent Staff

The three steps of good customer service according to Ritz-Carlton Hotel chains, which that are known for their quality customer service, are:

- Customer Step 1: Greet the patient using his or her name.
- Customer Step 2: Meet the customer's (patient's) needs.

- Customer Step 3: Wish the customer a warm farewell and use their name again, if possible.

While most of the medical offices cannot compare with the service in a hotel, in many offices, friendly, courteous patient service is not a priority. For example, try this simple test. When calling a health care organization, hospital, physician practice, diagnostic clinic, or practice, compare the responsiveness, training, personality, and professionalism of the person on the telephone with other businesses, say a hotel or even an airline. It is surprising how out of touch many health care businesses are with even the basics of telephone customer service.

Health care entities in recent years have undergone severe downturns, staff shortages, reduction in staff, and the inability to meet competitor's pay scales. Therefore, many practices find themselves unable to hire the staff members that they would choose. One of the ways that practices can improve their customer service is to discuss the specific image that the medical practice wants to project. Next, list the values that are expected of the staff. For example:

- How should the telephone be answered?
- How long is an acceptable length of time to place a patient on hold?
- Is the person answering the telephone knowledgeable in the aspects of directing the telephone calls?
- Do the appointment schedulers understand the appointment scheduling and the requirements of each of the tests and/or types of appointments that they are scheduling?
- Are billing personnel who deal with patients knowledgeable in answering questions regarding managed care, Medicare deductibles, and other pertinent payment issues?

Share the expectations with all staff members and make those expectations part of the annual performance evaluation. By focusing from the top down on providing friendly, courteous service to the patients, the practice should be able to meet this requirement.

Modern, Clean Office with Ample Parking

What does the décor say about the practice?[2]

- **External signage.** This is always a big issue because it can be so expensive to maintain. Look at all the signs that are used outside facilities. How easy is it to find a physician's office from all the routes through town? Do external signs make it easy to access the facility? Is the physician's name prominent on entrance signage? Are signs professional looking, in good shape, and lit at night?
- **Grounds.** What are the grounds and landscaping like around the facility? Are bushes and trees well pruned and maintained? Are people standing at the front entrance smoking? Are they staff members? What do the grounds outside say about the facility inside? What do they say about the staff?

- **Exterior facility.** What is the first impression the facility gives visitors and potential patients? Is it well maintained and modern or falling apart and out-of-date? Is the area well lit at night?

- **Internal signage.** How easy is it to navigate the facility? Are signs current and in good shape? Is the navigation process intuitive? Is natural design, light, and architecture used to support and direct movement throughout the facility? Are elevator signs easy to read and follow? Are there main directories, maps, and other support visuals?

- **Interior facility.** What is the first impression the facility gives from inside? What do the furniture, artwork, and general atmosphere say about how the practice wants customers to feel? What is the lighting like? What odors does the facility have? How noisy is the facility? How noisy are patient rooms and private areas?

Figure 7-1 can assist a practice in surveying their office.

FIGURE 7-1

Facility Checklist

FACILITY CHECKLIST		Yes	No
1.	Does the reception area look like a place you would be comfortable in?	❏	❏
2.	Are the magazines of interest to you?	❏	❏
3.	Are they current?	❏	❏
4.	Is the front desk free of clutter?	❏	❏
5.	Do you get the feeling that your medical information is protected?	❏	❏
6.	Can you overhear staff member's personal conversations?	❏	❏
7.	Is the temperature comfortable?	❏	❏
8.	Do signs give information in a positive manner?	❏	❏
9.	Are exam rooms comfortable?	❏	❏
10.	Would you be relatively comfortable wearing exam gowns?	❏	❏
11.	Are hallways free of clutter?	❏	❏
12.	Are there interesting pieces of artwork or pictures on the walls?	❏	❏
13.	Are medical instruments well organized/out of sight?	❏	❏
14.	Are staff members professionally dressed?	❏	❏
15.	Are you able to handle your bill in private?	❏	❏
16.	Are patient charts protected from accidental exposure?	❏	❏
17.	Is the office atmosphere calm? bustling? frenzied?	❏	❏
18.	Is entryway clean and welcoming?	❏	❏
19.	Is the parking area safe, convenient?	❏	❏
20.	Is signage to your office clear?	❏	❏

Error-Free Billing

Providing error-free billing goes back to having knowledgeable, competent staff members. Billing errors cannot only be a patient satisfaction problem, but they may also lead to compliance issues— a problem every medical practice should wish to avoid.

It is essential to have someone knowledgeable in billing matters to handle the telephone calls. If part of the errors in the billing originates at the front desk, as is often the case, then performance standards should be developed so that patient demographic and insurance information is correctly entered into the computer system and staff members are held accountable for that information. If the practice's computer system is difficult to work with, thus causing billing and instrument errors, then it will be worth the practice's investment to seek other resources.

Prompt Callbacks

Prompt callbacks with lab results and other patient questions go hand-in-hand with office accessibility. Patients want to be seen close to the time that they call and also expect to receive callbacks in a timely manner. For example, if policies are established that lab results be forwarded to the patient within 10 days, message callbacks be returned within 2 to 3 hours, and prescription refills completed the same day as requested, then patients should be made aware of those guidelines in order to manage their expectations. If there are more telephone calls, prescription refills, or calls for laboratory test results than the practice can reasonably handle, then the practice should take proactive steps to determine why the volume of calls is so high and determine a way to correct the problem.

PATIENT SATISFACTION SURVEYS

How does the practice know if patients are satisfied with the office functioning? One way is to ask them. When using a patient satisfaction survey, keep the survey simple, with no more than two sides and something that the patient can complete within 10 minutes. Offer the survey to every patient who comes into the office. When developing a patient satisfaction survey, try using a 4-point rating scale, such as "poor," "good," "above average," and "excellent" (see Figure 7-2), to measure the patient's opinions regarding:

- Ability to get a timely appointment
- Waiting time after arrival at the office
- Ability to reach the office by telephone
- Promptness in having telephone calls returned
- Courtesy of check-in receptionist
- Courtesy of medical staff
- Accuracy and timeliness of statements
- Courtesy and interest during the visit

Once the patients have completed the patient survey, identify the top one or two areas for improvement. These improvements can then be

FIGURE 7-2
Patient Satisfaction Survey

ABC HEALTH SERVICES—PATIENT SATISFACTION SURVEY

Please circle your physician's name

Charles X, MD	Arnold Y, DO	Janine Z, MD	Rebecca A, DO
Robert B, MD	Joy C, MD	David L, MD	Lisa M, MD
Sylvia N, NP	Other _____		

Please circle the answer that best represents your feelings. If you had no exposure to an item, skip the question. Please select only one (1) answer per question.

4-Excellent	3-Above Average	2-Average	1-Below Average	0-Poor

Appointment Scheduling

1. Were you able to schedule an appointment when you needed one?	4 3 2 1 0
2. Were you given options for appointment times?	4 3 2 1 0

Environment

1. Were the signs and directions to the office adequate?	4 3 2 1 0
2. Was the waiting area clean and orderly?	4 3 2 1 0
3. Was the examination room clean and orderly?	4 3 2 1 0
4. Was the waiting room reading material appropriate and current?	4 3 2 1 0

Patient Care Staff

1. Was the front desk staff courteous, friendly, and caring?	4 3 2 1 0
2. Was the nursing staff courteous, friendly, and caring?	4 3 2 1 0
3. Was the staff prompt in responding to your needs?	4 3 2 1 0
4. Were you treated with respect and dignity?	4 3 2 1 0
5. Was the staff concerned for your comfort and privacy?	4 3 2 1 0

Physician

1. Did the physician see you at your appointment time?	4 3 2 1 0
2. Was the physician courteous and caring?	4 3 2 1 0
3. Did the physician keep you informed about tests and treatments?	4 3 2 1 0
4. Were you given clear instructions, follow-up, and education on your condition?	4 3 2 1 0

Overall

1. How would you rate your overall experience with ABC Health Services?	4 3 2 1 0
2. Would you return to this facility in the future?	4 3 2 1 0
3. Would you recommend this physician?	4 3 2 1 0

Comments

What recommendations do you have for future services?

_____

_____

_____

Additional Comments (describe good or bad experiences)

_____

_____

_____

Thank you for taking time to complete this questionnaire. Your concerns are our priorities.

made by discussing the specific image that the medical practice wants to project and listing the values that are expected of the staff.

IMPROVING PATIENT SATISFACTION

Following is a list of suggestions for improving patient satisfaction:

1. Discuss the specific image that the medical practice wants to project. Hold a practice workshop where teamwork is discussed as the optimal practice enhancement tool.
2. Determine how marketing and patient satisfaction matter in the managed care environment and discuss proven methods of enhancing patient satisfaction (see Figure 7-2, Patient Satisfaction Survey).
3. Solicit patient feedback and concerns by using office comment cards and newsletters with comment feedback.
4. Organize patient focus groups.
5. Complete complaint logs.
6. Obtain unsolicited letters and comments.

SUMMARY

In the scheme of medical practice management, patient satisfaction is the ultimate long-term gauge of practice success. Patients who are satisfied with the care and treatment they receive are loyal to the practice; those who are not, often quietly slip away without ever expressing their dissatisfaction. Some may speak their minds so the practice can respond, but others simply leave. No marketing and practice-building effort compares to meeting the needs of patients and satisfying their expectations for respect and care. Happy patients are the most likely to come back again, send others to the practice, comply with treatment and recommendations, and pay their bills.

ENDNOTES

1. Blender R, Marey C. Are Your Patients Patiently Waiting? What to do About Patient Wait Times. *The Journal of Medical Practice Management*. 2001;2:16.
2. Fell D, "What's their first impression of you?" Health Marketing, Health Leaders.com, April 24, 2001.

RESOURCES

Blender R, Marey C. Are Your Patients Patiently Waiting? What to do About Patient Wait Times. *The Journal of Medical Practice Management*. 2001;2:16.

Bright S, Caldwell C. The Cost of Quality. Available at: Healthleaders.com, December 4, 2001, www.healthleaders.com/news/features. Accessed December 19, 2001.

Fell D. What's Their First Impression of You? Available at: Healthleaders.com, April 24, 2001, www.healthleaders.com/news/print. Accessed December 19, 2001.

chapter 8

Managing the Telephone

To many patients, if a practice manages its telephone calls well, that indicates it can also manage health care well. While this correlation may have little factual basis, the telephone usually does provide a practice's first impression.

HOW DOES THE PRACTICE SOUND ON THE TELEPHONE?

The most important meeting is the first, and a telephone call into the practice often serves as that first meeting. How does the practice sound on the telephone? The following questions may help with the answer:

- How promptly are the telephones answered?
- How courteous is the receptionist?
- How efficient is the receptionist at fielding the call (ie, Is the call for an appointment, prescription refill, or obtaining an answer to a medical question?)

How the practice views the telephone and its relationship with its patients will determine how well it meets the needs of the caller. In practices that put the needs of the practice first, telephone calls are likely to be answered and returned as it meets the needs of the practice and the staff (ie, patient calls are placed on hold or transferred until the staff has time to handle them).

However, in a patient-centered environment, every telephone call is viewed as a person with a need to be met, not just a voice. Calls are returned promptly and efficiently and a caller's permission is requested before moving him or her along in the communication process.

Surveys have shown that patients who have difficulty making appointments, contacting a physician, or obtaining care for an urgent problem are more likely to change practices. Therefore, to ensure the continued success of a medical practice, it is imperative that the practice learn to courteously, professionally, and, most of all, efficiently manage the telephone calls. It is important that each patient who encounters the practice comes away with a good impression.

The first moment of truth is when a patient calls the office. For that reason, it is important that the practice establish performance standards for anyone who answers the telephone and talks to patients. For example, performance standards might include:

- **Smile when on the telephone.** Smiling relaxes the face and makes one's voice sound friendlier. (Some practices place a small mirror at each telephone so that employees who answer the telephone can see themselves smiling at the caller.)
- **Establish a standard way to answer the telephone.** For example, 95% of all calls should be answered within three rings. The call will be answered in the following way:

  Good morning, (name of group). *This is* (answerer's name) *speaking. How may I help you?*

  This is a professional and courteous way to answer the telephone. (Regardless of the number of calls that the practice receives daily, answering the telephone should never be shortened to just "Doctor's office.")
- **Obtain the caller's permission to place the call on hold.** "May I place you on hold for a moment while I look up that information?" is a courteous way to inform the patient that they will be placed on hold. If the "hold time" extends beyond 30 to 45 seconds, it is courteous to let the person on hold know that the answerer is still working on the information. In such a case, give the patient the choice of continuing to hold or call them back.
- **Advise the patient of what is going on before transferring a call.** For example, "I'm going to transfer you to Beth in the clinical department. She will be able to assist you with that question." This lets the caller know what is about to happen, the reason for the transfer, and gives them the opportunity to respond or ask questions.
- **Use the patient's name during the telephone call.** This will help to establish a personal relation with him or her. Use Mr, Mrs, or Ms in talking with the patient. Never address patients by their first name, regardless of how long the patient has been coming to the practice.
- **Take accurate messages.** When taking a telephone message, always verify the spelling of the patient's name and the telephone number where he or she can be reached. Even the simplest names have variations on spelling. Verifying all information will eliminate errors that could prevent a return call.
- **Call the patient back.** If a patient must be called back with information rather than providing it at the time of the call, give the patient an approximate callback time and then call at that time.
- **Avoid using slang.** Try using words and phrases such as "certainly," "thank you," or "my pleasure," instead of "okay" or "thanks" whenever possible. Also, avoid using medical jargon that patients may not understand.

Managers can also improve the quality of the telephone service by conducting role-play sessions where staff members are given the opportunity to practice dealing with the angry caller, the demanding caller, the emergency call, and other common, but often difficult scenarios. Having well-trained personnel is the key to an effective and efficient telephone operation. It takes a different set of skills and knowledge to respond to a patient's medical needs (eg, appointments, prescription refills) versus a patient's billing and insurance questions.

MANAGING TELEPHONE DEMANDS

To the medical practice that is managing increased demands, the telephone often represents an obstacle to efficient practice management and a potential obstacle to patient relations. And, as patients become more active in their health care management, telephone usage is inclined to increase rather than decrease. Practices may find it almost impossible to keep up with this increased demand.

Some practices may find themselves continually adding telephone lines, telephones, and staff members to answer the telephone in an effort to keep up with patients' needs and demands. However, adding access to the office via telephone without addressing ways to manage this increasing demand will bring only short-term results. Patients may notice improved telephone service for a short period of time after the addition of lines or answerers, but demand usually quickly catches up with the increased access.

For this reason, the first step to improve telephone service is to manage the call and the call volume rather than to reactively add access. Managing call volume involves:

■ Reducing the number of calls coming into the practice
■ Reducing the time spent on each call coming into or going out of the practice

When faced with the questions "Is it time to add another line?" or "Do we need to hire more staff?", it is advisable to take time to analyze the telephone situation before making the investment in more lines or more people. To complete this analysis, it will be necessary to:

1. **Gather information.**   Most telephone systems are capable of providing reports that outline the number of calls that are received and the length of each call, as well as the time and date of the call. This will help the practice to determine when high-volume calls take place. Although most practices will readily say that they receive the most calls Monday morning, few will be able to go beyond that and say on what days and at what times patients are inclined to call. If the current system will **not** do this, then it is necessary for the practice to develop a data-gathering system (see Figure 8-1, Telephone Call Log). Although this puts increased burden on staff for a short time, it will provide the practice with telephone management information.

FIGURE 8-1
Telephone Call Log

TELEPHONE CALL LOG

Day _____
Date _____

	Appt. w/ doctor	Presc. Refill	Test Results	Talk to Nurse	Appt. for Other	Billing	Medical Records Transfer	Other
AM								
PM								

2. **Identify the types of calls and the volume.** Prescription refills, calls for the triage nurse, questions for the physicians, requests for appointments, and calls for test results should all be counted to determine the source of incoming calls.

3. **Start to change the demand.** Once the practice has gained and analyzed this useful information, start changing the demand. It may be found that some calls can be eliminated by proactively managing the flow. Highlight areas on the call log that can be managed and reduced. For example, calling patients the day after a procedure to see how they are doing may prevent the patient from calling in at a peak time to ask a question about his or her progress. Scheduling patients for their next visit at the time of patient check out will eliminate many future calls. Likewise, advise patients both verbally and with a supplemental handout that it usually takes 4 days to receive lab test results. This will prevent patients from calling the day after a test for those results.

4. **Arrange staff to meet peak levels.** By identifying peak calling times, the practice will also be able to arrange staffing to meet those busy periods. A part-time worker assisting with the telephone three mornings a week might be a better investment than adding more lines or more full-time staff.

5. **Handle each call efficiently.** Another way to manage the telephone is to handle each call as efficiently as possible. Obtaining poor or inaccurate information on the first call that necessitates making a second call is poor telephone management. Also, allowing a 5-minute telephone call to last for 15 or 20 minutes will also add to telephone problems.

When dealing with patients, many staff members find it difficult to provide good customer service while simultaneously keeping the call efficient and manageable. To assist staff members in telephone management, role-playing training sessions, along with scripts, will help them in their telephone conversations.

Training sessions might include finding ways to end the call gracefully, yet effectively. Such phrases as, "Have I answered all your questions before I go?" or "Just one more thing before I hang up" will signal to the caller that the call is terminating.

Often, the stage can be set at the onset for keeping calls short. Having all needed information at one's fingertips before placing a call will expedite the business of the call. Phrases such as, "I have three quick questions to ask you today" or "It's so nice to hear from you Mrs _____. How may I help you today" will move the conversation along to the intent of the call.

Another way to manage telephone demand includes logging telephone calls as to the nature of the call and the time spent on the call. This will help the staff member keep track of the time actually spent on the telephone. Business calls can turn into social calls when a well-known patient or colleague is on the other end of the telephone.

Personal Calls on the Business Telephone

The practice should have a strict policy about personal calls. A private line in the break room or in a quiet place might be reserved for staff calls during their break. If patients are complaining about receiving a busy signal every time they call the office and there is an average of four people on personal calls any time during the day, then the practice will continue to have a telephone problem. Getting staff members to respect the importance of keeping telephone lines open for patient calls is a high priority in telephone management.

Making Each Call Count

What starts out as an attempt to save the physician's time often turns into many calls by many different staff members to handle one patient's telephone call. Incomplete or unclear written messages from a patient's call, incorrect patient telephone numbers for callbacks, and misunderstood instructions often result in two or three calls to the patient rather than one. To reduce calls, triage nurses should be instructed to verify the spelling of the name of each patient for whom they take messages, along with repeating the telephone number back to the patient for accuracy. Physicians can help in this process by delegating callbacks to those staff members who will understand the nature of the call, have within the scope of their job description the authority to answer patient questions, and know when to give the patient an answer and when to defer the question to the physician.

The telephone encounter form in Figure 8-2 will help staff to systematically answer and document inbound telephone calls. Place a pad of these forms at key telephone stations where messaging and triage take place.

Many practices have dedicated telephone lines for prescription refill requests. Some channel these calls directly from an automated attendant or through voice mail. Patient education can be a valuable tool when it comes to prescription refills. Remind patients to bring any refill requests with them at the time of the appointment and include a refill policy in the patient information brochure to help eliminate frantic calls from patients from the pharmacy.

PROVIDING MEDICINE BY TELEPHONE

"Call back on Tuesday for your test results, Mrs John," "Call the nurse if you are having any problems," "Call us in 3 weeks for an appointment," and other "call us" instructions are said to patients hundreds of times a day in practices throughout the country. While giving patients the reassurance that the practice is there for them, these instructions also contribute to congested telephone lines, patient dissatisfaction, staff frustration, and potential liability risks.

One of the first steps practices can take to manage telephone demand is to take a proactive approach to calling patients on the

ABC Practice
1234 Medical Place
My Town, USA
(404) 123-4567

TELEPHONE ENCOUNTER FORM

Patient Name:

Date of Birth:

Medical Record Number:

Patient Identification

Date of Call: _____ Time: _____ ❑ Call Placed ❑ Call Received ❑ Call Returned

(Dept. Initiated)

Caller's Name: _____ Relationship to Patient: _____

Telephone
Number: Work _____ Home _____

Primary Physician: _____ Section Completed By: _____

Presenting Problem / Chief Complaint:

_____
_____
_____
_____
_____

Assessment (including current medications):

_____
_____
_____
_____
_____

Advice Given / Protocol Used: ❑ Call Back if No Improvement ❑ Return to Clinic / ER

_____
_____
_____
_____

Rx ordered: _____ Ordering MD: _____

Rx called in: _____ Pharmacy: _____ Tel #: _____ Time: _____

Disposition: ❑ Call for Appointment ❑ Appointment Made Date: _____ Time: _____
❑ Call in AM ❑ Return for Next Scheduled Appt. ❑ Advised Seek Emergency TX

_____
_____

Signature: _____ MD Signature: _____ Time: _____

practice's time schedule. Examples of ways a practice can take control of the telephone and effectively use it for managing a patient's medical condition are:

Jane will call you back within 10 days with your test results.

Please schedule your next appointment on your way out.

Here is a list of common questions patients have about your scheduled test, along with explanations. Take a few minutes and read them over and Jane will call you in a few days to see if you have additional questions we can help you with.

However, there will always be a need for the triage desk, the place where patients who need answers or help can receive advice over the telephone.

Some of the situations that have been shown to represent areas of potential high exposure to risk are:[1]

- The patient who calls back repeatedly and is not seen face-to-face
- The patient whose anxiety seems out of proportion to the symptoms (this includes anxious parents calling about their child)
- The pregnant patient with a concern
- Any patient who is uncomfortable with self-care suggested by telephone

Documentation of telephone encounters is as important as documenting face-to-face encounters. A useful tool to assist the nursing staff in documentation is a well-designed telephone encounter form, which features clinical prompts:

- Chief complaint
- Past and present history
- Pertinent positives and negatives
- Advice given
- Consultations obtained
- Expectations for follow-up

Clinical guidelines, including telephone management guidelines, are essential for nursing practice. They serve as a training tool and ongoing resource and become the nursing standards for the individual practice setting.

Answering services should be periodically evaluated for courtesy, efficiency, accuracy, and proper record keeping. By using unqualified answering service personnel, urgent messages can be delayed or patients can become discontented, often transferring their displeasure from the answering service to the physicians. Several courts have held a physician vicariously liable for the acts of an answering service. Office staff should have a list of emergency telephone numbers readily available.

USING TECHNOLOGY TO MEET TELEPHONE DEMAND

The technology solutions for telephone service and options are countless and can be mind-boggling. Before investing in equipment, software, or services, become an educated consumer through research of available options.

Automated Answering System

Many practices have found that the automated answering system or telephone tree has helped manage their telephone demand. While some patients may find that being answered with an automated "machine" is disconcerting, others will value the efficiency of being able to reach who they want without undergoing long waits, busy signals, or being placed on hold.

Before implementing an automated system, consider these factors:

- The same number of calls that are received now will continue to be received after the implementation. The automated system will only more efficiently direct those calls and prevent callers from receiving a busy signal.
- The voice directing the automated system needs to be professional, easy to understand, and friendly. It may be worth the expense to professionally record the message to improve patient acceptance and satisfaction.
- Telephone messages will still need to be returned—and promptly. Patients will very quickly learn to hate a system where calls go to a black hole of voice mail, never to receive a response. Fast and efficient responses to the calling patient will improve patient satisfaction and confidence in the system.
- Make the automated system user-friendly.
- Make instructions or medical emergencies the first option so callers can chose it quickly.
- Provide a range of options that are tailored to the most common needs of the patients. For example, "If you wish to schedule, reschedule, or cancel an appointment, press 2 now. If you wish to request a prescription refill, press 3 now. If you wish to request a referral, press 4 now."
- Limit the time a caller must spend with the automated attendant to less than 60 seconds.
- Educate the patients about the benefits of the system and how it works by displaying this information in the reception area and including it in the practice's newsletter, new-patient letter, and other communications.

Computer Telephony[2]

Often referred to as *computer telephony*, it is the technology associated with the electronic transmission of information using a computer via the telephone. It can help a practice expand customer contact, reduce incoming calls, increase staff efficiency, and improve customer service.

A typical telephony system does three things:

1. Processes an automated telephone conversation
2. Documents the calls
3. Uses external data to control the content of the communication

Many practices are discovering the advantages of using telephony to provide test results to patients, as well as confirming upcoming appointments.

Once the information has been properly entered into the system, patients will receive only correct information. The advantage is that patients will always hear a familiar, pleasant voice efficiently delivering needed information. Gone are the days of hurried or garbled messages delivered in a frustrated tone.

Most patient communication systems document all calls, providing reports for patient records. Also, all attempts to contact a patient are documented, thus reducing malpractice risks.

INVESTING IN A NEW SYSTEM

When the practice is ready to make a change in their telephone system, start by getting a clear picture of the current system's problems and compile a list of hopeful improvements with the updated or new system. Talk to the staff about what they want the telephone system to do. Try to think ahead; plan for the practice's growth and future needs. Keep in mind that a typical telephone system should last 5 to 10 years.

Consider sending a request for proposal (RFP) to a number of vendors. Having written proposals will help when comparing features, service, and price. Evaluate the proposals in light of the practice's needs. Each vendor will explain all necessary details. Take that information and educate the practice, then come up with a prioritized list of criteria for the new system.

Sample Criteria for a New Telephone System[3]

Here is a list of must-have features that private practices should consider when updating their telephone system:

1. Capacity to grow with the practice. For example, to add telephone lines when necessary and new features when available.
2. Voice mail, an automated attendant, a prescription-refill line, an intercom/paging system, 3-way calling, and a call-forwarding feature.
3. A separate telephone line from the main system that will work when the system is down.
4. An "emergency ring" feature (ie, all telephones have a distinctive ring to signal an emergency call received by the automated attendant).
5. A dedicated outside line for each telephone unit.
6. Dedicated lines for computer modems and fax machines.
7. Two or three telephones at each station in the clinic.
8. Technical support from the supplier (ie, a contract making the vendor responsible for getting the system back up and operating as soon as possible if it goes down).

Should the Practice Invest in a New System?

Once the practice has determined what telephone system features are wanted, determine if they can be added to the present system. Some telephone systems cannot support new technology, which may make it necessary to acquire a new system.

Purchase or Lease?

If the current telephone system must be replaced, the practice must determine whether to purchase or lease the new system. Compare the cost of purchasing, plus maintenance agreements, to those of a lease agreement. Also, compare upgrades and maintenance costs included or in addition to the lease. It may be cheaper to lease the equipment rather than purchase it and have to maintain it over time. Keep in mind that whether buying or leasing, the practice will still need to purchase individual telephone units and wiring for the office.

New telephone systems can cost several thousand dollars depending on features and the number of lines. The system can be paid for in one lump sum or financed over time. Most vendors will offer a 2-year warranty on the equipment, with an optional extended warranty. Expect to pay several hundred dollars annually for an extended warranty.

Be sure to get in writing what the vendor is responsible for covering and what the practice will be responsible for paying. Also, check vendor references and ask about response time to maintenance calls, expertise of staff, and quality of equipment.

Ask about On-Site Training

Even the best-designed telephone system will be useless if the staff does not know how to use it. The vendor should provide the initial training and be available to provide additional training in the future. Ask how many days the trainer will be on-site initially, how many times he or she will return to the practice if needed, and the cost of additional sessions.

SUMMARY

The telephone system and the way telephone calls are handled in the medical practice is a vital part of practice management. Equipment and technology that comprise a practice's system are key. Furthermore, staff members and telephone protocol are also fundamental to patient care. The practice must have an adequate system in place with a staff that is well-trained in answering and handling the many incoming calls and various outgoing information that are a part of the daily practice operations.

ENDNOTES

1. Hoffman J. The risks of patient encounters by telephone. *Journal of Medical Practice Management.* November/December 1998; 3.

2.   Baker LP. Communicate with patients using common office equip-
     ment. *The Journal of Medical Practice Management.* September/October
     1998; 2.

3.   Torrey B. Getting the most from your phone system. *Family Practice
     Management Journal.* February 2001. Available at: www.aafp.org.

RESOURCES

Baker LP. Communicate with patients using common office equipment. *The
     Journal for Medical Practice Management.* September/October 1998; 2.

Beck LC. *The Effective Front Desk Staff.* Conshohocken, Pa: Advisory
     Publications; 1997.

Flanagan L. How does your practice sound on the phone? *Family Practice
     Management Journal.* January 1999. Available at:
     www.aafp.org/fpm/990100fm/45.html. Accessed February 1, 2002.

Hoffman J. The risk of patient encounters by phone. *The Journal for Medical
     Practice Management.* November/December 1998; 3.

Sachs L. *The Professional Practice Problem Solver: Do-It-Yourself Strategies that
     Really Work.* New York: Prentice Hall, Inc; 1991.

Torrey B. Getting the most from your telephone system. *Family Practice
     Management Journal.* February 2001. Available at:
     www.aafp.org/fpm/20010200.21gett.html.

Woodcock E. The telephone: managing demand. *The Journal for Medical
     Practice Management.* July/August 1999;1.

chapter | 9

Appointment Scheduling and Patient Flow

One of the most important aspects of practice management is establishing an appropriate patient appointment schedule and facilitating the flow of those patients through the practice at maximum efficiency. Maximum efficiency, in this case, does not mean that patient satisfaction is not taken into consideration. Rather, it means that the more efficient the practice is at scheduling and seeing patients close to that appointment schedule time with the appropriate work performed, the more profitable the patient encounter will be for the patient, as well as for the physician.

DESIGNING THE SCHEDULING TEMPLATE

Every practice should design a scheduling template for maximum efficiency. When designing appointment schedules, consider the following issues:

- What are the practice's hours of operation?
- How early are physicians willing and able to begin seeing patients?
- How late will patients be seen?
- What modifications will be made for lunch time?
- What days and times will the physicians be in the office?
- Will physicians offer Saturday hours?
- Will physicians take a day off during the week?
- Will the physical constraints of the office prevent all physicians from seeing patients at the same time?
- Will hours need to be staggered to provide room for physicians to work?
- How will hospital/surgery scheduling be done?
- When will the physicians make rounds?
- Are there considerations for nursing home care?
- What days will physicians do surgery?
- What will be the start and end time for physicians and staff?
- When will staff be needed for these hours?
- How much and what type?
- Will overtime be involved?

117

- Will the office close or remain open during lunch time and how are patients scheduled around this?
- Will extended hours for patient convenience (ie, early morning, evening, Saturday hours) be added?
- How will the types of presenting problems be scheduled, including:
  - Established recheck
  - Acute new problem
  - Nonacute new problem
  - Procedures
  - Tests
- How will patient contact be handled?
- How many patients can the physician reasonably see in an hour?
- Will walk-in patients be accommodated?
- How will emergent situations be handled?
- How much time and which facilities are going to be needed to perform office-based procedures?
- How are follow-up visits going to be scheduled?
- What role is the telephone triage person going to have in appointment scheduling?

When designing appointment schedules, the practice needs to consider the demographics of its patient base, including age and socioeconomic status. For example, the elderly patient or the pediatric patient will probably take more time to process through a practice compared to the patients who are working age and relatively healthy. Poor socioeconomic conditions usually result in a higher no-show or cancellation rate, partly due to childcare or transportation restrictions or inability to pay for the scheduled visit. Practice location can also influence appointment schedules. For example, a practice located in a metropolitan area where rush hour traffic is a factor will need to consider potential delays for appointments during that time of the day.

Openings in the schedule are also needed to accommodate walk-ins and requests from referring physicians. In designing a workable, accessible practice appointment schedule, it might be advisable to complete a physician survey, such as the one in Figure 9-1. This survey will vary based on the number of physicians and the types of services provided. Complete a survey for each physician in the practice, as well as for any nonphysician practitioners.

Once the surveys have been completed for each physician, a master appointment template can be designed. Having a master template with set policies and schedules will help the practice manage its patient flow and allow for any knowledgeable staff member to appropriately book an appointment.

It will also facilitate identifying ahead of time possible provider/room conflicts or overbooking of resources. For example, if the practice has one ultrasound machine, it may cause delays if two physicians choose to perform ultrasounds from 9:00 to 12:00 on Monday mornings.

FIGURE 9-1

Physician Survey

Dr A		
Services Performed	**Scheduled Time**	**Day or Time Restrictions**
New patient visit	30 minutes	No
Consultation	45 minutes	No
Established patient visit	15 minutes	No
Procedure 1	30 minutes	Yes - 1
Hours Scheduled		

Monday   Start _____ First patient   Stop _____ Last patient _____

Tuesday   Start _____ First patient   Stop _____ Last patient _____

Wednesday   Start _____ First patient   Stop _____ Last patient _____

Thursday   Start _____ First patient   Stop _____ Last patient _____

Friday   Start _____ First patient   Stop _____ Last patient _____

Saturday   Start _____ First patient   Stop _____ Last patient _____

1 – Patient fasting; schedule mornings before 10 AM

Special Considerations
Consultation requests to be seen within 1 week for routine.
Will work in patients sooner on emergent basis.

The need for appropriate appointment scheduling cannot be overstated. Underbooking the physician will result in reduced revenues. Overbooking the physician will result in poor patient satisfaction and diseconomies of scale.

What to Avoid to Maintain Steady Patient Flow

The following issues should be *avoided* in order to maintain a steady patient flow through the practice:

■ **Canceling patients/rescheduling.** In recent years it seems that the habit of the practice rescheduling patients' appointments has become more commonplace. It may be due to an increase of employed physicians as opposed to physicians in their own practice. Whatever the cause, patients should not be canceled from their scheduled appointments unless there is a true medical or personal emergency. In those rare instances, every effort should be made to have another physician in the group see the patient for the scheduled appointment. Canceling patients puts a burden on the administrative staff and decreases patient satisfaction.

■ **Not having a schedule set up in computer far enough in advance.** This prevents staff members from booking revisits at the time of the patient appointment. This subsequently results in either placing the responsibility on the patient of calling the practice and possibly not seeing them at all for the revisit.

- **Permitting physicians to continually change their schedule.**
  During the formative or refining phase of schedule development,
  it will be necessary to change schedules to some extent to arrive
  at best efficiency. However, physicians who continually change
  their mind on how they want their patients scheduled increase
  scheduling errors.

TYPES OF SCHEDULES

There is no one best scheduling format for appointment scheduling.
There are, however, several defined schedule types, each with its
advantages and disadvantages (see Table 9-1).

While not right for every practice, open access appointment
scheduling is gaining acceptance throughout the medical
community. In open access appointment scheduling, the practice
starts its day with 50% to 75% of its appointment slots open. As
patients call in for emergent needs or to schedule appointments, they
are then scheduled and brought into the office that same day.
Proponents of open access appointment scheduling point out that
when patients are scheduled far in advance, they tend to not show
for their appointment or cancel when the problem is no longer
urgent. By allowing them to come in on the day that they need to
come in, the practice is able to better manage the patient flow and
address the emergent needs of its patients.

Open access requires thorough planning because its
implementation will affect all facets of the practice. It is important
that both physician and staff champions of the process are identified.
A task force should be formed, including representatives from all
constituencies in the practice. This task force becomes the planning
body for the process and serves as the guide through the
implementation process.

The implementation process has three phases: data analysis,
planning/preparation, and actual implementation. As part of the
process, a detailed action plan needs to be developed. The action
plan should include specific steps of the implementation process,
identification of the individual who is accountable for completing
each step, and time lines for completion.

It is critical that the task force frequently and continuously
communicate with other members of the practice during the
implementation. Open communication creates involvement
and buy-in, as well as an understanding of the goals and
expected results.

RELIEVING FRONT DESK BOTTLENECKS

In many offices, the patient flow is hindered by a bottleneck created
at the check-in desk, which can be due to several reasons:

- Patients arriving late for appointments
- With group practices, all physicians scheduling the same type of
  patients at the same time, causing check-in overload

T A B L E   9-1

Outline of Schedule Types

Type of Schedule	Advantages/Disadvantages
Typical Format	Every 15 minutes. Extra slots are allowed for procedures, physicals, annual checkups.
	Advantage: This keeps appointment scheduling simple and prevents extended template reconstruction if the physician wants to modify the schedule.
	Disadvantage: Since all time slots are the same length, there are no built-in helps for appointment schedulers. This increases training needs and can result in errors.
Wave Method	Three patients scheduled to arrive on the hour and the half-hour. The premise in wave appointment scheduling is that one patient will arrive early, one on time, and one will arrive late.
	Advantage: Can eliminate physician having to wait on tardy patient.
	Disadvantage: Patients can become upset if they learn they are one of three people scheduled for a given time.
Based on Needs	New patients and procedures scheduled in longer slots. Revisits are scheduled in shorter slots. These are built into the system. For example, at 9:00 AM every Tuesday morning, appointment slots are reserved for particular procedures that the office performs.
	Advantage: Assists staff members by readily identifying, for example, "complete physical appointments."
	Disadvantage: The time slots based on needs can become too rigid if staff members are not empowered to override the templates. A physician could be sitting idle because no complete physical is scheduled when three much-needed re-checks were not scheduled.
Open Access	Services are provided to the patient the same day as the request. This is "doing today's work today."
	Advantage: Those practices that have successfully transferred to open access scheduling find that patient satisfaction increases, staff is happier, and cancellation and no-show rates have been reduced.
	Disadvantage: Open access is not for every practice. If finding the patient chart in the practice is difficult, open access may exacerbate the problem. Also, it is important to have all physicians in the group on this type of scheduling. It usually requires hiring locum tenens or assistants to clean

- Failure on the part of the practice to address insurance and billing information prior to the appointment time, thus placing that responsibility on the check-in person
- Inexperienced or undertrained staff personnel working in that area
- Inappropriate front desk staffing—not enough staffing at the right time
- Slow computer system, which causes delays in the registration process

Many practices make it a policy to wait until a new patient arrives at the office to begin the information-gathering process. This means that not only is the patient asked to complete new patient information forms, but also to provide health insurance information. A patient that arrives at 10:15 AM for a 10:30 AM appointment will still be in the registration process at the appointment time. This will cause the physician to run behind, and affect patients for the rest of the day.

To alleviate this problem, a practice can take steps ahead of time by:

- Preregistering the patient on the telephone at the time of the appointment

- Mailing registration forms along with a patient information packet before the appointment

- Scheduling the patient for the appointment and following up with a call from a patient intake specialist to obtain the desired information

- Conducting special training sessions for newly hired front desk members to increase their front desk knowledge and help them process patients faster

- Having patients preregister on a practice's website

Figure 9-2 illustrates how check-in time at front desk shortens time spent with the patient.

FIGURE 9-2

Example of a Check-In Schedule

Scheduled Time		Actual Patient Care Time
9:00	S. Smith, B.P. Check	7 min.
9:15		
9:30	J. Chen, Pap Smear *(Actual visit times often shorter than scheduled slots)*	23 min.
9:45		
	R. Linney, Backache	11 min.
10:00	Y. Gillis, Asthma	9 min.
10:15		
10:30	C. Wilder, Physical	22 min.
10:45		
	J. O'Grady, Cough	5 min.
11:00	Same Day (M. Peters, Chicken Pox)	12 min.
11:15	B. Johnson, Headache NO SHOW	
11:30	Same Day (K. Mori, Sprained Ankle)	10 min.
11:45	Same Day (J. Simms, Nausea)	6 min.
12:00		

105 | **Patient Care Minutes**

In Figure 9-3, a typical patient flow is illustrated in the following six stages:

- **Stage 1:** The scheduling of the appointment
- **Stage 2:** The interim work involved
- **Stage 3:** Checking in the patient
- **Stage 4:** The patient encounter
- **Stage 5:** Checking out the patient
- **Stage 6:** Post-appointment processes

Scheduling

Scheduling a patient can facilitate steady patient flow if complete telephone registration is taken at the time the appointment was scheduled. Scripts can be prepared ahead of time to assist the staff members in obtaining the required information. Practice information can be sent to the patient prior to the appointment schedule. This information can address insurance and billing information, prescription-refill policies, and co-payment and referral policies.

FIGURE 9-3

Example of Typical Patient Flow

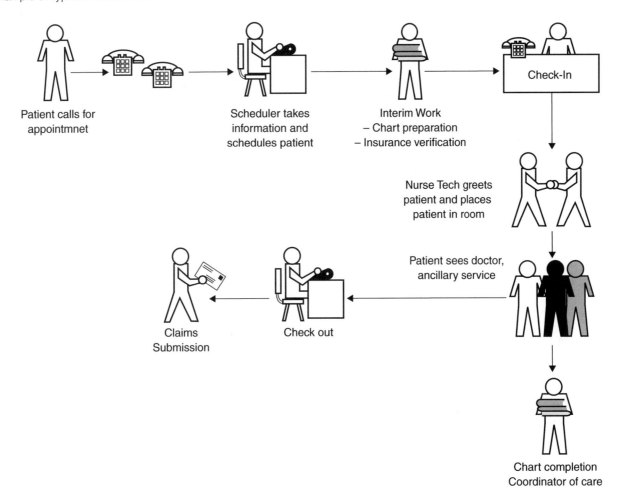

Interim Work

Of all the work that is performed for the patient encounter, the interim work is probably going to be the most beneficial to facilitating steady patient flow. Once the insurance information is obtained from the patient, the practice should verify eligibility of the patient for this insurance and determine the coverage of the services that are scheduled. Failure to do this ahead of time will only result in the practice having to follow up on this information after the service is rendered, and, in many cases, past service will not be paid for without prior approval.

Appointment confirmation can tremendously reduce the rate of no-shows and cancellations within a practice. Therefore, all appointments should be confirmed the day prior to the appointment time. A script can be designed for those individuals confirming appointments. During this call, patients can be reminded to check on their refill needs, referrals, and copayment responsibilities.

Records should be pulled 1 to 2 days ahead of time and stored on mobile carts in the practice. This will allow the practice to check the charts in advance to ensure that the patients' test results or consultations from other physicians are in the chart when they are needed. It is also a good idea at this time to see if there are any outstanding account balances that will need to be addressed.

Additional interim work for established, as well as new, patients is the chart preview. In this step, a nurse or other designated individual reviews each patient chart to determine that all paperwork necessary for the appointment is available. The chart preview form (see Figure 9-4) can be placed on the front of each chart to facilitate this review.

With preregistration information taken in advance of the patient encounter, when the patient presents to the check-in desk, the finalization of the updates in the system and advising the clinical staff that the patient is ready should take relatively little time.

BACK-OFFICE PATIENT FLOW

One of the most important necessities to steady patient flow is having approximately three examination rooms per provider. The physician can go from one room to the other without waiting and be able to see patients in an efficient manner. In order to do this, however, the practice must not only have enough examination rooms, but also staff that is able to keep patients moving in an efficient manner. One way to make the patient visit satisfying to the patient while keeping within the schedule is to ask the patient to complete an "Ask Your Doctor " card while waiting for their visit. The card helps them focus on the questions they want to ask their physician and, as a result, eliminates many repeat questions or telephone calls back to the office once they leave. See Figure 9-5 for a sample of an "Ask Your Doctor" card.

Other methods a practice can use to keep patients moving on time through the office are:

- Invest in a light signaling system that notifies the physician and nurse when a patient is ready to be placed in an exam room.

Example of a Chart Preview Form

CHART PREVIEW

Patient's Name _____ Account Number _____ Date of Appointment _____

☐ Complete Forms

☐ Demographics

☐ Consent

☐ History

☐ Copy of Insurance Card

☐ Insurance Verification

☐ Benefit Eligibility
☐ Recommended?   per _____
☐ Captured?   per _____
Insurance Co. Contact Name _____
Notes:

☐ Financial Counselor
☐ Recommended?   per _____
☐ Captured?   per _____

☐ Co-Payment $ _____

☐ Collect Payment $ _____

☐ Payment Plan $ _____

☐ Needs referral

☐ Needs referral if _____ ordered

☐ Laboratory tests

☐ Imaging (X-ray, MRI, CT)

☐ Referring physician correspondence

Example of an "Ask Your Doctor" Card

Your Practice Name
Questions to Ask the Doctor

Make the most of your time with the doctor.
Write down your questions for your doctor and any
needed prescription refills.
That way you'll be sure to cover everything while visiting the doctor!

Questions:

Prescription Refills:

- If a light signaling system is not available, use some messaging system that lets the physician know which room has the next patient.
- Limit physician interruptions by taking telephone messages rather than calling a physician out of a room. Prompt callbacks will make this an acceptable option.
- Assign a "flow manager" who is responsible for overseeing that the exam rooms are cleaned, stocked, and ready for the next patient.
- Plan ahead.

EMPLOYEE TIME MANAGEMENT

Have a "stand-up" meeting every morning for 10 minutes. Include the physician if possible. Following are sample topics that can be covered:

- Review the schedule for any special orders or circumstances.
- Give instructions to the staff for jobs that need to be done.
- Discuss with the physician any calls that were received or are expected.
- Get information from the physician that is required for accurate billing of services, diagnosis, or procedures done in the emergency room, hospital, or nursing home.
- Develop a *Practice Policies and Procedures Manual* that defines every job function. Have each employee contribute to the manual by providing an outline of his or her tasks/functions and how they are handled. Written policies and procedures are a great time-saver, excellent orientation and training resource, and a fundamental part of risk management.
- Encourage employees to use a daily "to do" list. Help them develop daily and weekly goals. Use the annual performance appraisal for helping employees set personal and professional goals for the coming year. Do not allow them to set goals and then forget about them. Rather, interface with them about their goals throughout the year. Continuously offer encouragement and praise; provide help only on request.
- Physician delays—Have a contingency plan prepared for when the physician is unavoidably detained (eg, hospital rounds, surgery). Notify the patients immediately; do not make them wait 30 to 40 minutes. A patient considers his or her time as valuable as the physician's time. Inform the patient of the anticipated delay and give him or her the option to reschedule.
- Telephone patients that are scheduled for the remainder of the morning/afternoon and let them know that they may be delayed. The patient may choose to delay his or her arrival time or reschedule the appointment for another day.

SUMMARY

Appropriate appointment scheduling and efficient patient processing is vital to acceptable patient satisfaction levels and the financial health of the practice. Gone are the days when patients waited quietly for 2 hours or more to see their physicians. Therefore, the physician who understands and values the patient's time as much as his or her own will be the physician patients want to see.

RESOURCES

Witt M. EZ Access: Delighting Patients with Same Day Service. Available at: www.epracticemanagement.org. Accessed on December 3, 2001.

Woodcock E. *The Five Principles of an Efficient Practice*. Glen Burnie, MD: Physician Practice Inc; 2001.

chapter 10

Managing the Medical Record

A well-developed medical record system protects patient confidentiality of sensitive issues and promotes quality patient care by accurately reflecting the patient's medical condition and services provided. Effectively managing medical records includes:

- Establishing efficient and consistent chart setup
- Accurately documenting patient's medical information and services provided
- Maintaining records in a safe and secure environment
- Protecting patient confidentiality in all transactions
- Maintaining records for an adequate length of time
- Properly destroying records

This is no small task, and it continues to grow as practices increasingly share information with other entities, bring technology into the practices that stores and transmits sensitive data, and continually change due to government regulations regarding the use and sharing of records.

WHAT IS A RECORD?

A record is nothing more than an account of an event preserved in a medium so that it can be read at a later date. Rule 803 of the Uniform Rules of Evidence, which has been adopted by more than half of the United States, focuses on business records, but its language is applicable to any record as being "a memorandum, report, record, or data compilation, in any form, of acts, events, conditions, opinions, or diagnoses, made at or near the time by or from information transmitted by a person with knowledge."

The federal Privacy Act, 5 USC §552a (1991), defines record as any item, collection, or grouping of information about an individual. Some states define the term *medical record*, while others merely specify what information such a record must contain. Some states provide detailed guidelines on what a medical record must contain; other states leave it up to the facility to define what a medical record comprises. In such an event, sufficient information to justify the diagnosis and warrant the treatment and end results probably is not sufficient both to provide proper health care and to minimize litigation losses.

Patient records of hospitals participating in Medicare must contain sufficient information to identify the patient and justify admission and hospitalization; support diagnoses; and describe the patient's progress and responses to treatment. Each record must also contain reports of physical examinations; patient's medical history; admitting diagnosis; results of consultative evaluations; documentation of infection or adverse reactions or complications; patient consent forms; patient monitoring information (ie, medication schedules, lab reports, radiology reports); and a discharge summary that includes a final diagnosis, disposition of the case, and follow-up provisions.[1]

WHO OWNS MEDICAL RECORDS?

What should health care facilities tell patients who demand their medical records, stating that the records are theirs? The fact is the health care facility owns the record and consequently has the right to physical possession and control. The patient has a right to the information contained within it. Many states have statutes specifying that the health care facility owns its medical records. Some states add that the facility's ownership is subject to the patient's right of access to the medical information contained in the record.

Even if the state statue or an administrative regulation does not specify who owns medical records, in the absence of a statute or court decision to the contrary, a facility may safely assume that it, not the patient, owns the medical records. Physicians practicing in a private office own their medical records, subject to rights of access by patients.

When a patient changes physicians (eg, when a physician leaves practice), the previous physician should transfer the records, copies, or summaries of the record to the current physician, although no strict legal duty to do so exists. Physicians who send patients to specialists have a legal obligation to provide the receiving facilities or physicians with all medical information from the records that is necessary to treat those patients.

WHICH RECORDS MUST BE KEPT AND FOR HOW LONG?

Health care providers must keep records for several reasons, namely:

- The law requires them to do so
- To provide better health care
- To minimize litigation losses

First, all levels of government have the undoubted authority to require a practice to keep records. Even if the law did not require a hospital or other health care facility to keep medical records, these records would still be necessary to provide proper care for patients. Attorneys who are involved in medical malpractice cases know that the most favorable situation for a plaintiff who is alleging medical malpractice is one in which the relevant medical records are lost, incomplete, or otherwise defective.

It is not hard to determine which records need to be kept, as federal, state, or local laws or regulations often instruct practices on these issues. Furthermore, once all required records are saved, practices often add even more records to their archives "just in case." The more illusive question is how long should a practice keep the various records. Even when a law provides for such a period or time frame, other considerations may require an office to keep the records even longer. Even worse, various laws may conflict. For example, a state regulation may provide for a longer retention period for a particular record than a federal statute. Practical concerns, like the availability of resources (eg, space and funding), will also affect the decision of how long to retain records. If the practice is uncertain about whether to keep a record, don't guess, check with an attorney.

POLICIES FOR MEDICAL RECORDS

To ensure compliance with HIPAA and other medical records regulations, a practice needs well-defined policies on who will have access to the record, what will be contained in the record, how records will be released to other parties, and how those records will be maintained.

Some of the policies a practice will want to include are those that mandate that:

1. A medical record be maintained for each patient treated in every setting
2. Each medical record in the organization contain, as applicable:
   - The patient's name, gender, address, telephone number, date of birth, height and weight, and the name and telephone number of any legally authorized representative
   - Legal status of patients receiving mental health services
   - Documentation and findings of assessments
   - Conclusions or impressions drawn from medical history and physical examination
   - Diagnosis or diagnostic impression
   - Evidence of known advance directives
   - Evidence of informed consent for procedures and treatments when required by organization policy
   - All diagnostic and therapeutic procedures, tests, and results
   - All operative and other invasive procedures
   - Progress notes made by authorized individuals, including the date, staff person, and care or service provided
   - All reassessments
   - All consultation reports
   - A medication list of all prescribed medications
   - Every dose of medication administered, including the strength, dose, or rate of administration; administration

devices used; access site or route; known drug allergies; adverse drug reactions; and patient's response to medication

■ All relevant diagnoses established during the course of care

■ Referrals or communications made to external or internal care providers and community agencies

■ When appropriate and necessary, treatment summaries and other pertinent documents to promote continuity of care

■ Documentation of clinical research interventions that is distinct from entries related to regular patient care

■ Any drug allergies

■ Signatures of treating or ordering physicians

3. All medical records should be completed promptly (within 24 hours)

4. All clinical summaries of treatment should be included in the medical record

5. Policies should be established that determine who is authorized to make entries in the medical records

6. The organization should also have a policy for the following:

■ Limiting access to medical records to those individuals authorized to make entries, or who are involved in care

■ Identifying the date and author of every entry in the record

■ Providing the author opportunity to authenticate an entry for completion and accuracy

CONFIDENTIALITY OF MEDICAL RECORDS

The flow of medical information carries numerous personal and societal benefits. The ability to access medical records has saved the lives of unconscious patients brought into hospital emergency departments. Pharmacists have detected dangerous, sometimes potentially lethal, drug combinations. In the public health arena, computerized records have made possible the prompt detection of infectious disease epidemics and enabled health authorities to take emergency action. Researchers have used databases to analyze the causes of illnesses, a process that, for instance, established the connection between smoking and lung cancer.

However, the vast accumulations of personal medical data give rise to serious privacy concerns as a result of the potential for misuse. The following are a few safeguards that were set up to ensure that medical records are kept private:

■ **Patient's right to know.**   Each patient, directly or through a representative, must have the right to know by whom and for what purpose his or her health care information is maintained.

■ **Restrictions on collection.**   Individual health care information must be collected only for legitimate purposes, such as medical research, enhancing public health, and combating fraud.

■ **Use of information.**   Health care information must be used only for necessary and lawful purposes.

- **Notification.**   Any entity maintaining health care information must prepare and make available to patients upon request a written statement outlining its information practices.
- **Restriction.**   Health care information must not be used for purposes other than those for which it is collected, except as provided by law.
- **Patient access.**   Each patient, directly or through a representative, must have access to his or her health care information and the right to amend or correct it.
- **Safeguards.**   Any entity maintaining individually identifiable health care information must be required to implement reasonable security safeguards.
- **Penalties.**   Both criminal and civil penalties must be provided for persons who violate privacy laws and regulations.

Probably the most effective way to ensure the security of the practice's records is to make certain the people who work with those records safeguard them. First, a careful screening of staff members who have access to critical or confidential records is a must. Once it has been established that the employees handling the records are responsible, the practice should promote security consciousness on the part of the staff by orienting new employees and refreshing old ones about the principles of record security and confidentiality. (See Figure 10-1 for the Medical Records Oath of Confidentiality.)

FIGURE 10-1

Medical Records Oath of Confidentiality

MEDICAL RECORDS OATH OF CONFIDENTIALITY

I, _____ do hereby swear and affirm that I will not discuss, reveal, copy, or in any manner disclose the contents of the medical record of any patient who has received or is receiving health care services from _____ _____ unless an appropriate and properly executed *Authorization for Release of Medical Information* form is received, and it is determined that the records are to be released to a person with a legitimate interest.

   I understand that medical records are confidential; that the information in a medical record is protected by both Federal and California state laws and regulations; and that reading, discussing, or otherwise utilizing the information within the record for other than legitimate health care purposes is grounds for immediate dismissal and possible legal action.

Sworn before me this _____ day of _____ 20____ at _____, California.

_____
Signature of Staff Member

_____
Signature of Administrator of Oath

Medical records may be destroyed in one of two situations—pursuant to the record retention plan or on a one-time basis. The latter is often necessary to eliminate old, worthless medical records that a retention program does not cover. Because courts look on any records destruction that is not part of a records retention plan with suspicion, the practice must be certain that the one-time destruction is properly conducted.

When it is time to destroy records, a practice cannot just take them out and throw them away. A lot more is involved. If the practice is conducting a one-time destruction of a group of records, rather than destroying records pursuant to the records retention program destruction schedule, the records must first be reviewed to make certain that they should really be destroyed. An excellent technique is to send out notices to interested parties, such as hospital directors, staff attorney, and the like, stating that the named records are going to be destroyed. If there is not response from the notices within a certain amount of time, the records can be destroyed without further discussion.

State or federal statues or regulations will normally prescribe how the records must be destroyed, usually by burning or shredding. Often, the controlling law will require the practice to create an abstract of any pertinent data in medical records prior to destroying them.

If a commercial document destruction company is used, the practice should do so under a contract that sets forth how to destroy the records; how to avoid breaching confidentiality, including indemnification from loss due to unauthorized disclosure; and how the practice will glean the required documentary proof of the destruction.

What is done with the records when a health care facility ceases operation, either because another facility acquires the facility, it merges with another facility, or it closes?

Some states have statutory or regulatory guidelines that tell practices what to do if a facility closes or merges with another facility. If not, the practice may want to contact the local medical society or a health care attorney.

SUMMARY

Maintaining and handling medical records in a way that compiles patient information as a resourceful tool and protects patient information as private documentation is a significant and ongoing exercise for the medical practice. Every practice must have orderly systems and policies in place and ensure that the guidelines and routines are consistently followed during the course of patient care and for many years following.

ENDNOTES

1.   42 CFR §482 (1990).

RESOURCES

American Health Information Management Association. Confidentiality of Medical Records: A Situational Analysis and AHIMA's Position. Available at: www.ahima.org.

Joint Commission on Accreditation of Healthcare Organizations. The 2000–2001 Self-Assessment Checklist: Ambulatory Care. Oakbrook Terrace, Ill: Joint Commission on Accreditation of Healthcare Organizations; 2000.

Murphy BJ. Principles of good medical record documentation. *The Journal of Medical Practice Management.* March/April 2001;5.

Tomes JP. Healthcare Records Management, Disclosure & Retention: The Complete Legal Guide, New York: McGraw-Hill, 1994.

chapter 11

Integrating Technology

Increased patient record keeping requirements, patients who access information on medical information through the Internet, restrictive drug formularies, and staff restriction has forced physicians to look for solutions. For many physicians, that solution has come through technology.

WIRELESS TECHNOLOGY

New products are being introduced daily, both in the software market and in hardware with the introduction of new devices and gadgets. In addition to those products created specifically for health care professionals, other technology, such as handheld devices, cell phones, and web-based products, can assist physicians and managers in performing their jobs more efficiently.

Security and Privacy

With increased use of technology in maintaining and transmitting patient medical information comes increased concern for privacy and security. Even without the implementation of the Health Insurance Portability and Accountability Act (HIPAA), patients and physicians historically have had concerns about the security of health information that was being electronically transmitted. HIPAA addresses those concerns and outlines methods in which health care entities must comply to protect personally identifiable health information (PHI) from access by unauthorized persons or organizations. Physicians need to carefully select wireless devices for HIPAA compliance.

ELECTRONIC MEDICAL RECORD (EMR)

EMR solutions are rapidly becoming accessible to even the smallest medical practice in response to the need to:

- Improve the ability to share patient record information among health care providers
- Improve clinical processes or workflow efficiency
- Improve quality of care
- Provide access to patient records at remote locations
- Improve clinical data capture
- Facilitate clinical decision support

- Improve patient satisfaction
- Improve efficiency via previsit health assessments and postvisit patient education
- Support and integrate patient health care information from Web-based personal health records
- Retain health plan membership[1]

From a clinical perspective, EMR systems can help address:

- The need to share comparable patient data among different sites within a multientity health care delivery system
- The requirement to contain or reduce health care delivery costs
- The need to improve clinical documentation to support appropriate billing service levels
- The need to establish a more efficient and effective information infrastructure as a competitive advantage
- The need to meet the requirements of legal, regulatory, or accreditation standards
- The need to manage capitation contracts (eg, global capitated contracts, specialty carve-outs, subcapitation for medications, hospitalization.)[2]

However, not all EMR systems are created equal. For example, on the one side, some systems, calling themselves EMR, are actually little more than word processing systems that have little or no integration capabilities. On the other end of the spectrum, fully integrated systems can accommodate all aspects of a patient's records, including radiology films, hospital records, laboratory results, and prescription refills. These systems can even track them, as well as generating an accurate and complete bill and integrating with the physician's handheld device for hospital charge capture.

In fact, so much capability is available that physicians and managers often become confused and overwhelmed as they try to select the best product for their practice.

There are almost 200 vendors that offer EMR capabilities, and the list is growing daily. Increasingly, more physicians are looking at an electronic system to help them manage the office paper flow. However, converting to an electronic system is no simple task. Questions that need to be addressed before the search for a new system begins include:

1. How much integration do we want? Are we talking about a way to manage the practice's records or are we hoping to incorporate X-rays, lab results, and prescription refills?
2. Do we want voice-based, pen-based, screen pad, or written entry of information?
3. Are we envisioning a computer in every exam room, only in the physician's office, or a notebook that the physician can carry around?
4. Is every physician in the group in favor of this move and willing to use the technology?

The survey in Figure 11-1 can be used to gather information from each provider in the practice to determine the group's readiness to move to an electronic system.

FIGURE 11-1

Example of an EMR System Survey Questions and Responses Form

EMR System Survey Questions and Responses

Physician Name:	(optional)

1. **I use a computer at home:**
   - Never
   - Once per week or less
   - 2 to 4 times per week
   - 5 or more times per week

2. **I use a computer at work:**
   - Never
   - Once per week or less
   - 2 to 4 times per week
   - 5 or more times per week

3. **I use, or have used, the following types of software (check all that apply):**
   - Word processing
   - Spreadsheet
   - Statistics
   - Graphics
   - Database
   - Presentation

4. **I use, or have used, the following operating systems (check all that apply):**
   - Apple McIntosh
   - Windows
   - DOS
   - UNIX

5. **I am comfortable using a mouse (input device):**
   - Yes
   - No

6. **When recording text, I generally:**
   - Type faster than I handwrite
   - Type slower than I handwrite
   - Type and handwrite about the same speed

7. **I regularly use (at least once per week):**
   - Book/journal on-line databases
   - Library catalog on-line databases
   - Electronic mail
   - Hospital network services (eg, lab test results)
   - CD-ROM reference books or databases
   - World Wide Web
   - Electronic prescription service

8. **In my current position, I have professional patient contact approximately _____ % of the week:**
   - None
   - 0 – 50%
   - 50 – 100%
   - 100%

(continued on next page)

FIGURE   11-1

Example of an EMR System Survey Questions and Responses Form—*continued*

9. **When recording a patient encounter, I usually:**
    Dictate the record
    Handwrite the record
    Type the record to paper
    Type the record to a computer
    Both dictate and handwrite record

10. **I believe that using a computer for record keeping and to access information during patient examination will:**

    Decrease record keeping time:
    Agree
    No effect
    Disagree

    Improve accuracy of records:
    Agree
    No effect
    Disagree

    Allow more time to interact with patients:
    Agree
    No effect
    Disagree

    Intimidate most patients:
    Agree
    No effect
    Disagree

    Compromise patient record security:
    Agree
    No effect
    Disagree

    Negatively affect the doctor/patient relationship:
    Agree
    No effect
    Disagree

11. **I believe that the following, if true, would be significant advantages of electronic medical record keeping (check all that apply):**
    Ability to search past records
    Statistical evaluation/research capabilities
    Drug-interaction checking
    Recall patients for preventive care
    Ability to access databases or services, such as:
    Literature citations
    Drug information
    Hospital network
    Referring physician lists
    Electronic mail
    Online reference materials

FIGURE 11-1

Example of an EMR System Survey Questions and Responses Form—*concluded*

12. **I believe that the following, if true, would be significant disadvantages of electronic medical record keeping (check all that apply):**

        Capital cost of equipment

        Lack of mobility of input site

        Keyboard data entry

        Learning or training time required

        Disruption of patient encounter

13. **Do you think your office staff would embrace the change to an EMR system?**

        Yes

        No

APPLICATION SERVICE PROVIDERS (ASPs)

For small- to medium-sized practices that have not invested a lot in information technology (IT) infrastructure, entrusting IT systems to an application service provider (ASP) may be a safe answer, as well as a realistic one.

The ASP Question

The major dilemma in choosing an ASP is finding the right solution from among the many options. The first step is to define the requirements and then discover which ASPs meet those requirements. One resource available on the Internet is a directory at www.aspnews.com. There are several ASPs to choose from at this site, but choosing is where the challenge really begins. The practice must be certain that information can be synchronized between the different ASPs.

For large physician networks or hospitals the context is different, but in the end the problem is the same. Larger networks have already spent extensively on building and administering their underlying infrastructure, and they cannot simply bundle it all up and send it to an ASP for hosting. However, large entities can capitalize on the ASP trend by relying on the new breed of service providers to handle some specific applications. For example, it makes sense for a large physician group to consider using ASPs for automating their practices through computerized patient records (CPR) or electronic medical records (EMR) technology. In doing so, large corporations can leverage ASP expertise without an enormous initial investment and, most importantly, stay current with the latest application upgrades. All of this seems great, right? Well, it would be if it were not for the sticky question of integration. How can a practice synchronize information handled by an ASP with in-house applications or other applications within the health system?

This is where enterprise application information (EAI) comes in. EAI is not just a matter of integrating software packages and in-house developed applications. In fact, when dealing with ASPs, it is one of the most important keys to success.

Addressing the EAI Issue

EAI is a major aspect of ASP, but it can also be very confusing. EAI issues may apply each time the practice attempts to integrate applications. Solutions do exist. Extensible Markup Language (XML) is one of the leading solutions, but it is not necessarily for all purposes. XML is quite common today as a computer language standard.

With evolution and pressures from HIPAA to standardize the various methods of communicating and ensuring patient privacy, the medical field will eventually see EAI issues becoming less of a problem. However, it is critical that all the applications speak the same language or are able to convert to the same language through integration. Otherwise, the practice will likely be disappointed with an ASP and unable to capitalize on having a complete Enterprise solution.

VOICE RECOGNITION SOFTWARE

Many physicians look to voice recognition software as the solution to their dictation/medical records problems. The concept is that the physician can dictate directly into a computer and thus bypass the transcriptionist and file clerk. Voice recognition systems require training the software to understand and correctly enter the dictated information. Inappropriate words and misunderstandings require the physician to back up and correct the error. Voice recognition technology is continually improving and integration capabilities are increasing.

Voice recognition systems are used primarily in Windows-based technology and relieve the burden of transcription costs. However, not all physicians have the time or patience to work with and develop a voice recognition system to its fullest capabilities. If considering a system, think about the following:

■ How much integration is available with the system? Does the system print out a patient record? Does it maintain a record in the database? Will it fully integrate with laboratory, billing, and pharmacy?

■ Does the physician have the patience to work with the system for 2 to 4 months in order to get it fully functional?

■ How much time is this going to take for each patient visit?

When getting demonstrations for voice recognition software, avoid relying on vendor's demonstrations to determine speed, accuracy, and ease of use. By asking to be allowed to dictate a document before the demonstration begins, the physician will have a better idea of how the new instrument works.

HANDHELD DEVICES

Although less than 1% of physicians have technical power at their fingertips, estimates are that that figure will increase to 20% within the next 5 years.[3] Handheld devices can aide physicians in capturing charges as they make hospital rounds, selecting the appropriate codes, and checking for drug interactions. The cost of handheld devices continues to decrease, while more sophisticated features and programs are available. Overall, handheld devices are a relatively inexpensive way to give physicians the latest technology.

E-MAIL

Physicians and practices are increasingly relying on the Internet for communications with their patients. This trend reduces telephone calls coming into the office and allows a systematic approach to dealing with patient questions. When using e-mail, enhance the communication by:

1. Letting patients know in the practice's patient brochure and on their Web site what purpose the e-mail will serve.
2. Stating a response time for a submitted e-mail message.
3. Providing policies for managing e-mail after hours.
4. Telling patients to call the office for the quickest response. E-mail is not intended to be the emergency department or a method of quickly contacting the physician.
5. Asking patients to identify themselves in the body of the message.
6. Letting patients know who will be reading their message.

What's In It for Me?

An Intel study indicates that increased communication between physicians and patients through the Internet is not only satisfying to patients, but may reduce unnecessary office visits by as much as 25%.[4] When office visits are reduced, patients with urgent needs have increased access to care. The Internet provides an attractive alternative to the inefficient method of telephone tag.

WEB SITES

A well-designed practice Web site can function as an information tool and marketing tool for the practice along with improving patient satisfaction and reducing telephone calls to the practice.

Not only can the Web site provide photographs of the physicians and their credentials, but it can also give driving directions to the office, offer answers to most frequently asked questions, and provide patient education. Investing in a well-constructed Web site will pay for itself in the staff time it takes to answer the questions.

USING THE INTERNET—APPROPRIATELY—IN THE MEDICAL OFFICE

While the Internet has become a valuable resource for medical office managers and other staff members, it is not without its problems. Once Internet access is made available to individuals, new management issues appear.

Questions such as, "Can I monitor what staff members access?" "Can I be held responsible if an individual accesses adult-content sites?" and "How can I make sure Internet privileges are not abused?" are just a few examples of questions managers must face.

The practice's personnel policy manual should include policies on Internet usage, outlining limits on personal use, prohibited Web site usage, and protection of the practice's name and code of ethics.

CELL PHONE USE IN THE MEDICAL PRACTICE

Widespread use of cellular service is becoming a major problem in public places, particularly to those who are forced to overhear both personal and business dialogue conducted within earshot. Surprisingly, in the medical practice, some physicians and clinical staff are finding patients reluctant to terminate conversations on a cell phone during an exam, while receiving injections, while undergoing tests, and while going through procedures.

Consider the following questions:

1. When does a patient's liberty to talk on the cell phone override the responsibility not to impose personal conversations on unwilling listeners?
2. Does the patient have the freedom to interrupt patient flow by detaining the physician while he or she waits for the patient to terminate a call?
3. What is the physician's responsibility to see that patients do not interrupt patient flow or hinder care by conducting telephone conversations during an office visit?
4. Does the patient cause unnecessary risk to the practice by not interacting during treatment or while receiving an injection?[5]

Although the practice may be hesitant to introduce cell phone usage policies to their patients, it may be in the best interest of the practice to do so, particularly as use becomes more prevalent.

SUMMARY

Today's technology can greatly increase a practice's compliance, regulatory requirements, and the coordination of patient care among many providers. Having patient information readily available to the physician at the time of the encounter can facilitate the decision-making process and reduce the risk of errors or inappropriate treatment.

However, along with the advantages of this readily available information comes the ethical and legal responsibility for safeguarding that information. HIPAA regulations require medical practices to have security standards in place for any personally identifiable health information that is electronically transmitted.

ENDNOTES

1. What are the major management/administrative factors that are driving the need for Electronic Health Record (HER) Systems? *Medical*

Records Institute. 2000. Available at: www.medrecinst.com/resources/survey/2000. Accessed on January 23, 2002.

2. Ibid.

3. Graham S. Wireless Breaking into Healthcare Field. Available at: www.bizjournals.com. Accessed on January 5, 2001.

4. Baum N. Use e-mail to communicate with your patients. *MGMA Medical Update.* February 15, 2001:3.

5. Stanley K. Cell Phone Use in the Medical Practice. *The Coker Group.* Available at: http://www.cokergroup.com/CokerConnection/newsletter Vol1No4PartA.htm.

RESOURCES

Baum N. Use e-mail to communicate with your patients. *MGMA Medical Management Update.* February 2001.

Daigrepont J. Selecting an EMR vendor. *Coker Connection 2001;*1(6).

Daigrepont J. Identifying your ASP. *Coker Connection 2001;*1(4).

Krotz, D. A Town Goes Digital. *Health Leaders.* January 2002.

Leppoff, O. Wireless invasion: healthcare's evolution to wireless connectivity. *The Journal of Medical Practice Management 2001;*16.

What are the major management/administrative factors that are driving the need for Electronic Health Record (HER) Systems? Available at: www.medrecinst.com/resources/survey/2000. Accessed on January 23, 2002.

chapter 12

Financial Management

Concerns with multiple payer requirements and increased regulatory oversight often distract physicians and managers from normal business activities and delay monitoring practice revenues and expenses. Then, when bank funds reach an alarmingly low threshold, or when they find themselves waiting on the incoming mail to see how much money they brought in that day, budgeting, expenses, and revenue management once again is given its due attention. Practices can take steps to avoid cash shortfalls by developing an operating budget, knowing the cost of delivering goods and services, and preventing misappropriation of funds.

THE OPERATING BUDGET

The practice's operating budget is based on an annual average of operating expenses. The practice should be able to plan the spending requirements as they directly relate to their earnings. The budget will allow for preplanning and will provide the ability to curb needless spending and unplanned purchasing.

The importance of an operating budget cannot be overstressed. The basic concept is to:

- *Review* historical collections and spending
- *Plan* how much money can be spent in the coming months
- Attain an *acceptable* level of cash reserves

Financial success depends on the knowledge and understanding of the complete financial workings of the practice. This includes knowing the cost of each service that is delivered and the average cost of seeing each patient.

Do not be discouraged about the budgeting process. While it may be perceived as too complicated or time-consuming, the method that follows is a straightforward process.

ESTABLISHING THE BUDGET

One way to budget is to look at what better performing practices in a specific specialty spend on selected categories and strive to reach those averages. When using this method, the expenses of one practice are compared to those of other practices in a specific specialty nationwide. By doing so, a practice can discover which areas need work to reduce various costs and glean some tips for reducing those costs.

To begin, gather the following documents:

■ The most recent year-end financial statement or the last 6 months report annualized.

■ A copy of the Practice Management Statistics form (Figure 12-1). This form should be used at quarterly intervals so that peaks and valleys in the practice's operation expenses and earnings can be gauged.

■ The Major Expenses by Specialty table (Table 12-1) shows the national averages for major expenditures in each specialty. If information from another source specific to a region is available, use those benchmarks. These statistics are provided annually by a number of sources. The data in this table is from the Medical Group Management Association.

■ To determine how a specific practice compares to the benchmarks, calculate the total expense-to-earning percentage. Divide total expenses in any category by total collections or revenues. Check the benchmarks to see where the practice stands.

For example, if gross collections are $450,000 and salary and wage expense (excluding physician salaries) is $80,000, personnel costs are about 18% of collections. Notice in Table 12-1 that the national average ranges from 16.82% to 25.59% depending on specialty for staff salaries.

Once all the expenditure percentages have been calculated, enter them on the Practice Management Statistics Form (Figure 12-1). Then

TABLE 12-1

Major Expenses by Specialty

Expense Category	Cardiology	Family Medicine	GASTRO	Internal Medicine	OB/GYN	Ophthal.	ENT	Pediatrics	Surgery General	Orthopedic
Total Employer Support Staff Costs	17.78%	25.59%	17.55%	24.10%	21.10%	22.86%	17.78%	22.69%	16.82%	18.27%
Personnel Benefits (included in total Employee Support Staff Costs)	4.58%	5.72%	4.80%	5.46%	5.03%	4.37%	3.92%	4.)57%	4.30%	4.37%
Rent	4.40%	7.00%	5.12%	6.65%	6.17%	6.80%	6.75%	6.33%	5.21%	5.75%
Lab	0.38%	3.33%		4.82%	0.49%					0.21%
Medical Supplies	1.32%	3.95%	0.46%	2.80%	2.96%	1.35%	2.03%	12.16%	0.69%	2.62%
Administrative Supplies	1.31%	1.90%	1.45%	2.26%	1.66%	1.80%	2.21%	1.89%	1.63%	1.54%
Information Technology	1.60%	1.51%	1.59%	1.72%	1.71%	1.39%	2.03%	2.26%	1.90%	1.38%
Malpractice	1.00%	1.49%	0.97%	1.28%	3.59%	0.81%	1.65%	1.08%	4.27%	2.06%
Legal and Accounting	0.86%	0.76%	0.69%	0.70%	0.85%	1.05%	1.10%	0.70%	0.70%	0.79%
Promotions/Marketing	0.40%	0.32%	0.35%	0.33%	0.74%	1.88%	0.56%	0.25%	0.41%	0.63%
Operating Overhead	45.67%	56.08%	39.81%	58.89%	50.12%	51.24%	48.88%	57.65%	39.56%	45.09%

Source: Used with permission from the Medical Group Management Association,104 Inverness Terrace East, Englewood, Colorado 80112-5306; 303-799-1111. www.mgma.com. Copyright 2001.

FIGURE 12-1

Example of a Practice Management Statistics Form

		My Office			
Category	**National**	**1st Qtr.**	**2nd Qtr.**	**3rd Qtr.**	**4th Qtr.**
PRACTICE MANAGEMENT STATISTICS FORM					
Collections:					
Total annual collections					
Refunds					
Net collections					
Managed care collections					
(List each major plan separately.)					
Expenses:					
Total expenses					
Total overhead percentages					
Salaries (%)					
Medical supplies and drugs (%)					
Administrative supplies (%)					
Occupancy expense (%)					
Malpractice insurance (%)					
Legal and accounting (%)					
Practice Statistics:					
Staffing ratio					
New patient visits/week					
Established patient visits/week					
Revenue per patient visit					
Cost per patient visit					
Average new patient charge					
Average established patient charge					
Collection Ratio:					
Accounts receivable ratio					

place the national averages for the practice's specialty on the form. Target the areas that exceed the national average.

While benchmarking is a helpful tool, it only provides information about the average practice. The national statistics do not account for the various ancillary services provided by some practices, which have a significant affect on revenue production.

National statistics, specific to a specialty, can be obtained through the Medical Group Management Association and through other sources.

Major Expenses by Specialty

Table 12-1 provides 2000 data that enables one practice to compare its expenses to other practices in the same specialty. The information is based on *national averages* and is intended for use only as a guideline. The physician's practice philosophy and the complexity of the practice may alter these averages for each specific practice.

Once a practice's standings are compared with industry benchmarks, a realistic budget for that practice can be determined. Determining the annual budget means taking a realistic look at the practice's proposed revenues and expenses and comparing actual performance to benchmark amounts on a regular monthly or quarterly basis.

Remember, the financial picture is a comparison of expenses to revenues. To improve the percentage in any category, the practice must either improve revenues or reduce expenses. Accounts receivable management is discussed in Chapter 13, Billing and Collections.

MEDICAL AND ADMINISTRATIVE EXPENSES

Medical and administrative expenses make up the bulk of a practice's monthly budget after personnel salaries, benefits, and rent. To reduce medical and administrative expenses in identified areas, review the suggestions outlined in the following sections.

Purchasing

Supply costs are generally a large expense in a medical practice and an area where there is almost always room for improvement. After reviewing the national averages and comparing costs, consider the following tips for cost reduction:

- Institute an employee suggestion box for cost-cutting ideas. Give a *prize* each month for the best recommendation that actually saves the practice money. Keep the staff involved by letting them decide which suggestion is best.
- Take advantage of free items. Pens, pencils, note pads, and even personalized prescription pads are provided by almost every pharmaceutical sales representative and other vendors.
- Eliminate frills, such as buying four types of pens to suit various employees.
- Ask the staff to concentrate on saving money in supplies for a specific period. If expenses are measurably reduced, reward them with a special treat, such as lunch or a small bonus.
- Consider joining a purchasing club or service. Group discounts may be available by buying with others in quantity.
- Purchase at the best possible price:
  - Ask medical supply vendors to charge the hospital price.
  - Consider ordering generic goods rather than brand-name items.

- – Order nonsterile, loose, multipacked dry goods in bulk.
- – Buy at year-end.

■ Conduct price comparisons every 6 months. List the items most often used and circulate this list to the vendors of choice. Include the size and quantity of each item.

■ Identify suppliers who provide the best quality for the money (eg, local manufacturers, discount houses, catalog purchasing).

Outsourcing

As medical practices are increasingly burdened with administrative paperwork, outsourcing offers a popular alternative to adding personnel. The decision to outsource may reduce administrative headaches and save money in the process.

Outsourcing is not really new. Many practices outsource various accounting functions, such as billing and collections and payroll.

■ **Billing and Collections**.   Many practices hire an outside agency to provide these services on a percentage basis. When considering agencies for better collection results, select one that bases its cost on collections rather than charges.

If the practice is considering a change or upgrade in the computer system to accommodate billing functions, first investigate the possibility of outsourcing the billing and collection functions. The fees for these services are usually 5% to 10% of total collections. The cost of doing this work in house will most likely exceed 10% in addition to the cost of a new or upgraded computer system.

■ **Payroll.**   The payroll function is easily outsourced to companies that specialize in automated payroll processing. Because of volume and sophisticated computer systems, they provide these services at a fraction of the cost of handling the payroll and the associated tax functions in house.

Vendor Relations

Establish relationships with reliable, service-oriented vendors who offer good products at fair prices. Open accounts with businesses that will work with the practice on cost reductions for bulk purchases and drop shipments.

Order bulk purchases at year-end if possible. Sales representatives will offer the best prices at that time in an attempt to reach year-end sales quotas. Be familiar with price breaks for regularly used items so that they can be purchased in quantity at a discount.

Create vendor files by company name and file all invoices and statements alphabetically in chronological order.

Keep stock closets locked and off limits to vendors. Most sales representatives are honest; however, occasionally one will report that the practice is low on a particular item and order more, even items that are seldom used.

Inventory Control

Every office should have an inventory control system for all purchases, from office supplies to laboratory and X-ray supplies. A good inventory system not only increases efficiency but controls costs. Establish a supply inventory control system to:

- Prevent ordering supplies that are already on hand
- Prevent overordering
- Reduce the high volume of shelved goods

Most practices have some supplies that have been around for years that are seldom used. Know what is used and how much, and order only when supplies are needed. Have an office supply *roundup* at least twice a year. Clean out every desk and closet, gathering pens/pencils, paperclips, pads, and so forth. Use up all of those supplies and do not order unnecessarily.

Order Point System

To establish an inventory control system, try the simple Order Point System to control the amount of inventory on hand, minimize overstocking, and prevent shortages (see Figure 12-2). To use this system, first determine the following:

- The quantity of material or inventory item used in a 30-day period
- The time between order and receipt of goods
- The quantity of item needed during the period of time required in #2
- The level of buffer stock necessary in the event of an interruption of supply

Ordering Logs

Use order logs to track the date an order was placed for supplies, the quantity, and the cost quotes for each item. Consider the following:

- Cross-check packing slips with order log entries. Cross-check monthly statements with packing slips.
- Note in the log when a generic form of a product was ordered.

Occupancy Expense

The practice may not be able to do much about rent expenses unless it is the end of a lease period and office space is abundant. As the renewal date approaches, negotiate for a lower rental fee, or at least strive for no escalation. If rent is extremely high and the practice has extra space, consider office sharing arrangements or adding ancillary services to make the most of the space.

Save money on utilities. Heating and cooling bills can be reduced by using an electronic thermostat that automatically adjusts the temperature at predetermined times. Raise or lower settings according to the seasonal changes. Insulate windows to keep the controlled air inside. Insulate the hot water heater. Use the same cost-saving ideas that are used in the home, at the office.

FIGURE 12-2

Inventory Control Exercise

Example:
1. The office uses 100 5cc syringes per month.
2. It takes 12 days from the date of order to the date of delivery.
3. The office uses about 50 syringes in 12 days.
4. The office should have a buffer stock of 100 syringes in case of backorder.
5. The office should reorder when inventory reaches 150 syringes.
6. If 5cc syringes come 100 to a box, the office should tag the next-to-last box with a sticker that says, *Order Now.*
7. The office will use 50 syringes before the order is delivered, and will have a safety stock of at least 100 syringes when the new order arrives.

Malpractice Insurance

Research and negotiate malpractice policies every year. While this is time-consuming, it may save money. Rates vary among insurance carriers, so be sure to compare equivalent coverage.

Legal and Accounting Fees

If the practice pays an outside accountant for monthly financial statements, several thousand dollars each year may be spent in accounting fees. Consider having statements prepared by the accountant quarterly rather than monthly. If possible and financially inclined, prepare monthly statements in house. Purchase an accounting software package for the practice's computer that will allow for the preparation of financial statements.

Service Contracts

Examine the practice's service contracts to see if they are needed and worth the cost. Contracts on highly reliable equipment are a waste of money. Fax machines, telephones, personal computers, calculators, and high-quality laser printers seldom malfunction. Often, service contracts cost more than repair or replacement of the equipment. Avoid long-term service contracts or those that renew automatically. If contracts are paid up, take advantage of perks, such as routine maintenance and cleaning.

Petty Cash

Establish a petty cash fund (eg, usually $50 to $100) to pay incidental expenses. Begin by drawing and cashing a check. Place the cash with a designated employee who is authorized to disburse the fund according to guidelines and restrictions for the amount and purpose. When a disbursement is made, a designated employee records the details on a receipt form. The signature of the payer is obtained, and the completed form is initialed. When the petty cash fund is reduced to a predetermined amount, it should be replenished to the original amount (see Figure 12-3).

Establish a few ground rules for the Petty Cash Fund:

- The Petty Cash Fund is not to be used for cashing personal checks
- Every disbursement must have a receipt to back it up
- Do not use the Petty Cash Fund to make change
- Use a disbursements form to track petty cash spending
- Designate one person to be in charge of petty cash
- Maintain funds and receipts in a locked box
- Do not allow borrowing from the Petty Cash Fund

FIGURE 12-3

Sample of a Petty Cash Fund Disbursement Log

| Date Starting: _____ | Starting Amount (A): _____ |
| Date Ending: _____ | Ending Balance in Account: _____ |

DISBURSEMENTS LOG		
Date	**Reason**	**(A) Amount $**
Total Transactions: _____		**Total (B):** $ _____

| Request for Petty Cash: $ = (A) | Formula Starting Amount (A) − (B) = (C) |
| Your Name: _____ | Date: _____ |

Tracking Revenues

Successful revenue management requires the practice to have in-depth knowledge of the sources of revenue. This information may be available on a report generated by computer software called *Revenue by Financial Classification*. This report should be as finite as possible. Sort information by each major managed care contract and by Medicare and Medicaid. Know how much each managed care contract contributes to the practice's revenues to see how much revenue is at risk if the contract is lost.

Determining Profitability

Look at each deliverable service from an expense standpoint. Review lab and X-ray costs compared to collections from these areas. Also, factor in personnel costs.

Calculate the average cost for seeing a patient to enable the practice to determine the profitability of each contract. Unless the costs for treating each patient are known, the practice cannot successfully negotiate a fee. Use Figure 12-4 to determine the cost and revenue per patient.

Revenue and Expense

Expenses fall into two categories: *fixed* and *variable*. To determine the cost of seeing each patient, the practice is only concerned with variable expenses.

Fixed expenses remain the same regardless of patient volume. Examples are:

- Rent
- Equipment leases
- Salary and benefits
- Utilities
- Dues and subscriptions
- Taxes

FIGURE 12-4

Sample of a Patient Care Analysis Form

Patient Care Analysis Form

1. Total number of patients seen for prior 12 months . . . . _____

2. Total of all expenses for prior 12 months . . . . _____

3. Subtract from line 2 all fixed expenses (eg, rent, salaries and benefits, insurance, utilities) . . . . _____

4. Total patient expenses (variable) for prior 12 months . . . . _____

5. Total receipts for prior 12 months . . . . _____

6. Divide line 5 by line 1 to get gross revenue per patient . . . . _____

7. Divide line 4 by line 1 to get cost per patient . . . . _____

8. Subtract line 7 from line 6 to get revenue per patient . . . . _____

Variable expenses vary with patient volume. Examples include:

- Medical supplies
- Office supplies
- Lab fees
- Transcription services
- X-ray supplies

ASSET MISAPPROPRIATION

With a primary focus on maximizing reimbursement and controlling expenses, health care entities often overlook one of their most vulnerable areas within their organizations—the misappropriation of assets. Unfortunately, those who work with medical practices (as well as businesses in other industries) for any length of time are apt to face this predicament. Fraud and abuse costs US organizations more than $400 billion annually, and the most costly abuses occur in organizations with less than 100 employees (ie, $120,000 annually). The median loss for the health care industry is $105,000 annually.

Asset misappropriation frequently originates with dissatisfied employees or those who take advantage of lapses in internal controls. Many of the steps for internal controls are irrelevant to the financial performance of the practice, yet when ignored, they can result in significant losses to the practice. Furthermore, owners of private practices experience losses directly from their own income.

Internal theft and employee fraud have increased in virtually all industries in recent years — including health care organizations and medical practices. Employees from all levels can be imaginative in "beating the system."

Watch for early warning signals of misappropriation of funds, which can be classified in three major areas: (1) skimming, (2) larceny, and (3) fraudulent disbursements.

RECONCILING THE DAY'S ACTIVITIES[1]

One consistent problem for medical practices is the lack of controls over the closing out and reconciliation of each day's activity. This includes all of the charges that were incurred and posted, including all collections for the day that were received and posted on the same day. Failure to reconcile usually means that actual deposits will not match recorded receipts in the medical software billing system, which is a very important internal control element that helps prevent embezzlement. Proper closing out and reconciliation ensures that the practice is posting its charges each day on a timely basis. This allows the office to bill (and therefore collect) these charges on a timely basis. Use Figure 12-5 as a form to help reconcile the practice's daily financial activities.

FIGURE 12-5

Daily Reconciliation Statement

Daily Reconciliation Statement

Business Date: _____

Batch # _____

Total Charges	$ _____	**Batch Report Total**	$ _____
Cash	$ _____		
Checks	$ _____		
Credit Cards	$ _____		
Total Deposits	$ _____	**Batch Report Total**	$ _____

Mail Payments   Batch # _____

Total Deposits	$ _____	**Batch Report Total**	$ _____

SUMMARY

Regardless of the demands placed on the physicians' and managers' time, financial management issues must be addressed on a consistent basis. Too many practices have found themselves upon hard times because, despite the physicians' hard work at bringing revenues in, no one was watching the expenses going out. Financial management cannot be delegated — not to an accountant, a consultant, or even a manager. Physicians who want a successful practice can solicit help from others, but a good understanding of the financial workings of the practice is essential to success.

ENDNOTES

1. Tinsley R. Reconciling the day's activities. *Health Niche Advisor.* May 2000; 21.

RESOURCES

Medical Group Management Association. *Major Expenses by Specialty: MGMA Cost Survey 2001 Report (based on 2000 data).* Englewood, Co: Medical Group Management Association, 2001.

Reiboldt M. Asset misappropriation. *Coker Connection.* 2002; 2.

Tinsley R. Reconciling the day's activities. *Health Niche Advisor.* May 2000; 21.

chapter 13

Billing and Collections

Prompt billing and collections is essential to the financial success of the practice. This chapter offers accounts receivable management techniques and provides valuable tools for successful collections.

REVENUE

The revenue cycle is the single most important source for improving financial performance of a physician's practice. The cycle does not start when the patient reaches the checkout desk with bill in hand. It actually begins weeks, months, or even years before when the practice created its financial policy.

FINANCIAL POLICY

The *financial policy* is a written document used to educate staff members to policies and protocols, educate patients to comply with those established practice collection policies, and maintain revenue and income balance. Every practice should have a written financial policy that addresses the following issues:

- Expectations for payment at time of service (PATOS) of any part of the service that is the patient's responsibility. This includes:
    - Consistent collections of co-payments at the time of service, whether at the time of check-in or checkout. Collection of co-payments is an integral piece of the managed care agreement.
    - Collection of patient portions of the bill, including deductibles and payment for noncovered services
- Timely submission of claims.
- Handling of rejections and denials from payers.
- Appealing denied claims process and the reemphasis on collecting all funds due the practice.
- Handling special circumstances, such as:
    - Litigation cases where other parties are involved, such as workers' compensation, auto accident, and other accident cases
    - Collecting services on a minor when the accompanying parent is not the responsible party
    - Dealing with a patient who has been sent to collection
- Courtesy and professional discounts or prohibition of them.

REVENUE CYCLE

Many factors influence a practice's revenue cycle. Managed care penetration, payer mix, physician productivity and ability to capture all legitimate charges, front desk and billing office staff's knowledge and expertise, and internal office policies can all affect the revenue cycle. Managed care and federal regulations are *external revenue cycle* factors that have frustrated many practices into believing they have no control over revenue cycle improvement. Improvement in the *internal revenue cycle* — which is controlled by the practice — will typically result in a 5% to 15% increase in net collections.

External Revenue Cycle

All health care providers are facing payer trends that have decreased net revenues and require additional effort to ensure proper and timely payment. Some payer trends that have been identified are:

- Converting to payment-based or a fixed-fee schedule for procedures
- Reducing fee schedules or not providing annual increases
- Denial and/or *bundling* of claims to reduce payments to providers
- Slowing the payment cycle

In addition, HIPAA legislation, standardization requirements, and government regulations have resulted in added operational costs. Although practices have limited control over these external factors, they do have some leverage. Practices can drop plans that consistently delay payments or deny legitimate claims. Lowered reimbursement schedules and bundling of services are other tactics that practices should carefully monitor. Many practices erroneously believe they need to belong to every managed care plan to be competitive. The reality is that if it is costing more to deliver the service than the reimbursement for the service, the plan is not beneficial.

Even those managed care plans that do have reasonable fee schedules need to be closely monitored. Every insurance company will make mistakes, including those with good intentions. Some claims will be thrown out, some will be paid lower than the established fee schedule, and some charges will be dropped altogether. Therefore, what may look like poor payment from the insurance company is merely failure to monitor the payments that are being received.

Every payer should be monitored and reports run to look at the overall reimbursement the practice receives from individual plans. From those assessments, the practice can then determine with which plans they want to continue an agreement or which ones they want to terminate.

Internal Revenue Cycle

The internal revenue cycle offers a practice more control over the billing and collection process then the external revenue cycle. The collection process may be broken down into three phases of the billing revenue cycle: (1) preappointment, (2) appointment date, and (3) post-appointment process.

Phase 1: Preappointment Process
The preappointment process sets the groundwork for a successful patient encounter. This phase consists of:

- Patient scheduling and registration
- Eligibility verification and authorization
- Financial counseling

To ensure a successful patient encounter, the appointment must be appropriately scheduled and accurate and complete demographic and insurance information must be obtained from the patient at the time the appointment is set (see Figure 13-1). A successful encounter also involves counseling the patient regarding insurance carrier responsibilities and the patient's expected financial obligation.

Once the appointment has been set and the insurance information obtained, the practice should then set up processes for determining eligibility and verification of the treatment. This can include asking for the patient's deductible, whether or not it has been met, whether or not the services that have been scheduled are covered, and if the patient is a member in good standing.

Finally, any financial counseling that can be done regarding the patients' responsibilities and obligations can be conducted via telephone prior to the appointment time. Waiting until the patient is in the office to discuss services that are not covered by the insurance carrier leads to poor patient satisfaction, as well as a loss in revenue time.

Phase 2: Appointment Date Process
The appointment date process involves verification of the patient information (ie, both demographic and payer responsibilities) or confirmation of work that has been done beforehand. Explaining procedures that are to be performed to the patient and/or responsibilities should be part of the check-in process. Collecting co-payments at the time of check-in or checkout is also an important part of managing this revenue cycle. Patients should be educated on the fact that co-payments are due and payable at the time of the service and are not eligible to be billed in a regular monthly statement. Capturing all charges for the services rendered is an important part of the revenue cycle and may involve a review of the office encounter form, review of the codes that are currently in use, and educating the physician and staff. Appropriate use of modifiers and supporting diagnoses are absolutely essential aspects of improving the billing process. Figure 13-2 can assist a practice in obtaining the most amount of revenue for services rendered by educating the physician to accurately capture all charges.

Phase 3: Post-Appointment Process
The post-appointment process includes accurate and timely data entry, error reports prior to submission of claims, and follow-up with payers and patients for remittance. This third phase also includes

FIGURE 13-1

Example of an Insurance Verification Form

Insurance Verification Form

Patient Name: _____ Date: _____

Birth Date: _____ SSN: _____

Patient Relationship to Subscriber: _____

Employer Name: _____

Employer Address: _____

_____

Benefits Coordinator: _____ Telephone: _____

Insurance Carrier: _____

Plan Name: _____ Plan #: _____ Group #: _____ Policy #: _____

Type of Plan: _____ Traditional 80/20 _____ HMO _____ PPO _____ Other: _____

Mail Insurance Forms to: (Carrier or Employer)

Billing Address: _____

_____

Contact Person: _____ Telephone: _____

Renewal Period—Medical Benefits and Limits are Renewed on (M/D/Y): _____

- **BASIC COVERAGE**

Physician Payment Schedule: _____ UCR _____ RBRVS _____ Other Data

Percentage of COB (ie, 80/20): _____ % Insurance Coverage _____ % Patient Co-payment

Annual Outpatient Deductible: _____

Amount of Deductible Remaining: _____

Maximum Benefit: _____

Noncovered Diagnostic Services: _____

- **DIAGNOSTIC COVERAGE**

Percentage of COB (ie, 80/20): _____ % Insurance Coverage _____ % Patient Coverage

Annual Outpatient Deductible: _____

Amount of Deductible Remaining: _____

Maximum Benefit: _____

Noncovered Diagnostic Services: _____

- **MAJOR MEDICAL COVERAGE**

Annual Outpatient Deductible: _____

Amount of Deductible Remaining: _____

Maximum Benefit: _____

Noncovered Services: _____

FORM USED: _____ Company-Specific Form _____ HCFA-1500 _____ Electronic Filing

NOTES: _____

_____

_____

FIGURE 13-2
Example of a Charge Capturing Checklist

Charge Capturing Checklist	Yes	No
Is encounter form reviewed and updated annually?	❏	❏
Do physicians understand Evaluation and Management coding and documentation?	❏	❏
Do schedulers understand what services are covered by insurance carriers and when they need to get a release signed by the patient?	❏	❏
Does the practice have a tool for capturing charges in hospitals and nursing homes?	❏	❏
—Is it used consistently?	❏	❏
Do nursing and ancillary staff understand their role in the charge capture process? (ie, injections, technical procedures)	❏	❏
Does the practice account for all encounter forms at the end of the day to ensure none are lost?	❏	❏
Do physicians and posters understand CPT code modifiers and when to use them?	❏	❏
Do physicians and staff understand special Medicare "G" codes and when they are appropriate?	❏	❏
Is there a defined process for obtaining Advance Beneficiary Notices (ABNs) or waivers?	❏	❏
Is there a process in place to link the appropriate diagnosis code to the procedure to support medical necessity?	❏	❏
Are *bundled* services identified for each payer?	❏	❏
Are encounter forms manually totaled at conclusion of posting and checked against computer?	❏	❏

rejection processing, appeals and denials follow-up, and credit balance adjudication. When the preappointment task is compared with the post-appointment processes, staff can then see the importance of thorough verification and gathering of information in Phase 1. Therefore, any of the services that can be moved from the post-appointment to the preappointment process will help the practice manage its revenue cycle.

ESSENTIAL FRONT OFFICE FUNCTIONS

The following functions are essential to the management of the front office:

■ Obtain proper new patient intake information to include completion of forms and requirements for previous medical records appropriate to patient visit.
■ Obtain referrals, precertifications, and authorizations.
■ Review appointment schedule in advance of patient visit; note any co-payment and patient responsibility amounts for office collection.

- Maintain current and complete patient demographic and insurance information; obtain copy of insurance card(s) on each active patient.
- Complete insurance verification, with periodic updates.
- Confirm insurance eligibility dates.
- Enter appropriate comments into computer system.
- Track limited authorizations and referral numbers.
- Assure that the *advance* notification, out-of-network, and noncovered waivers, when applicable, have been reviewed with the patients and signed.
- Provide financial counseling to all patients prior to any treatment.
- Be aware of special accounts, such as bankruptcy, estates, and research.
- Code services to highest level of specificity with appropriate documentation.
- Maintain up-to-date medical records to support patient charges.
- Complete charge entry in an accurate and timely manner.
- Provide each patient with a receipt for all payments made at the office.

MANAGING THE REVENUE CYCLE

In order for a practice to efficiently manage its revenue cycle, it must know their payers and for what they will pay, know their indicators to gauge their progress, and know their performance so that it can be weighed against benchmarks for comparison.

Know the Payers

One of the surprising aspects of practice revenue management is how many practices do not know what they are supposed to be receiving from managed care organizations, what those managed care organizations will pay for, or any special coding, billing, or other requirements those organizations require. Therefore, to most effectively improve financial performance, it is important to develop a managed care matrix that:

- Outlines the major managed care plans
- Determines who in the practice is credentialed on those plans,
- Decides what preventive services the plan will cover,
- Highlights which laboratory, radiology, and hospital the patients can be referred to, and
- Offers other specialty-specific coverage issues.

Once the matrix has been developed and each person involved in the revenue cycle is furnished a copy, the authorization, charge capture, and provider information will be at the staff's fingertips. Figure 13-3 provides an example of a managed care matrix.

FIGURE 13-3

Example of a Payer Matrix

XYZ PRIMARY CARE

	All Credentialed	Lab	Radiology	Hospital	Preventive	EKG	PFT	Inject.	Supplies	Special Precert. Requirements
Managed Care 1										
Managed Care 2										
Managed Care 3										
Managed Care 4										
Managed Care 5										
Medicare										
Medicaid										
Commercial 1										
Commercial 2										

In addition to the managed care matrix, the practice should also develop reporting mechanisms to determine from where their patients and their payments are coming. This can be accomplished by running a report of all active patients by payer type. By doing so, managers will be able to pinpoint the payer with the largest volume of patients. This will help the practice make decisions regarding managed care contracts and marketing directives.

The second report that the payer mix will show will indicate the source of the revenue dollars. Here again, this may or may not coincide with source of the patients. Therefore, it is very important for a practice to know where both their patients and the revenue dollars are generated.

Having these two pieces of information will enable the practice to forecast future revenues and volume. For example, if the practice report indicates that 52% of the patients come from Medicare, 10% from Medicaid, 15% from Managed Care Plan 1, 12% from Managed Care Plan 2, and 11% from other sources, then, from the predicted volume of patients to be seen in the coming year, the practice will be able to determine the expected revenues.

Know the Indicators

Revenue cycles are managed with a series of reports that can be compared to benchmark numbers. A careful eye on these indicators will alert the practice to possible problems in the revenue cycle and direct the attention to where improvements need to be made. Typically, practices run a series of monthly reports that will tell them how much they charged, how much they have received, what their write-offs were, and, of the accounts outstanding, how long have they been outstanding and which payer owes them for those outstanding accounts. Additional reports can be run that will show claims that have been denied, claims that are outstanding, and other information that is specific to the practice management system.

To effectively manage the billing office, the practice needs to know their indicators. Therefore, it is advisable to run a battery of reports that will give the practice consistent information on a monthly basis, namely:

- Charges, receipts, and adjustments report
- Aged account analysis
- Aged account analysis by payer
- Denial report
- Collection report

While it is important to look at these reports on a monthly basis to determine how the practice is comparing to the previous month, it is also important to bear in mind that vacations, flu season, and other external factors will influence how the practice performs on a month-to-month basis. Therefore, in addition to running monthly reports and reviewing them, it is recommended that a practice trend their reports over a 13-month period (see Table 13-1). These 13-month trend reports will help the practice look at the big picture regarding practice performance and even out the spikes and valleys of practice reactions to short-term external factors.

TABLE 13-1

Thirteen-Month Performance Trend Analysis Table

	2001 January	February	March	April	May	June	July	August	September	October	November	December	2002 January
Total Charges	$651,278	$634,315	$698,251	$599,929	$645,359	$704,989	$589,444	$704,187	$683,729	$758,724	$768,665	$668,573	$830,454
Total Adjustments	$223,099	$256,370	$265,506	$253,448	$240,401	$226,546	$233,229	$235,871	$219,562	$274,092	$315,009	$321,080	$329,688
Total Collections	$354,205	$411,957	$419,542	$436,915	$415,243	$396,163	$432,945	$424,225	$375,452	$426,381	$411,587	$387,756	$424,338
Capitation Payment	$70,468	$74,427	$72,840	$73,594	$71,487	$69,711	$68,234	$71,912	$69,506	$70,983	$70,330	$69,266	$70,088
FFS Charges	$490,017	$466,830	$512,652	$434,710	$479,182	$538,950	$431,906	$528,618	$512,931	$584,786	$636,308	$497,821	$623,999
FFS Adjustments	$193,714	$167,545	$157,116	$168,341	$153,422	$139,452	$160,268	$146,716	$131,451	$176,216	$257,861	$224,374	$211,696
FFS Collections	$281,990	$333,297	$342,333	$356,804	$336,044	$317,218	$348,367	$337,812	$292,766	$350,319	$336,377	$313,710	$336,697
Gross Collection Pct.	54.39%	64.95%	60.08%	72.83%	64.34%	56.19%	73.45%	60.24%	54.91%	56.20%	53.55%	58.00%	51.10%
Net Collection Pct.	82.72%	109.00%	96.95%	126.10%	102.54%	82.80%	121.54%	90.59%	80.89%	87.98%	90.73%	111.59%	84.74%
Adjustment Percentage	34.26%	40.42%	38.02%	42.25%	37.25%	32.13%	39.57%	33.50%	32.11%	36.13%	40.98%	48.02%	39.70%
FFS Gross Collection Pct.	57.55%	71.40%	66.78%	82.08%	70.13%	58.86%	80.66%	63.90%	57.08%	59.91%	52.86%	63.02%	53.96%
FFS Net Collection Pct.	95.17%	111.36%	96.29%	133.95%	103.16%	79.40%	128.25%	88.46%	76.74%	85.74%	88.88%	114.72%	81.66%
FFS Adjustment Percentage	39.53%	35.89%	30.65%	38.72%	32.02%	25.87%	37.11%	27.75%	25.63%	30.13%	40.52%	45.07%	33.93%
Total FFS A/R	$960,194	$944,108	$990,158	$973,023	$927,227	$984,634	$907,961	$946,808	$1,034,663	$1,095,033	$1,144,422	$1,111,659	$1,185,302
FFS Days In A/R					#REF!	60.65	57.06	58.24	63.64	64.07	63.71	62.68	63.04
Aging													
Current				$372,696	$374,755	$392,661	$355,059	$407,910	$417,003	$454,249	$481,767	$386,280	$533,498
31–60				$190,837	$157,168	$180,758	$150,131	$170,461	$219,325	$211,124	$204,931	$241,106	$167,040
61–90				$99,687	$85,373	$97,792	$87,258	$76,315	$101,211	$122,870	$120,736	$104,934	$110,163
91–120				$69,746	$64,600	$62,500	$56,195	$47,667	$54,521	$63,983	$83,553	$90,641	$73,368
121 +				$181,379	$201,249	$220,208	$227,452	$216,574	$215,122	$215,072	$222,191	$255,002	$270,117

Know the Performance Indicators

Once the reports have been run, the practice can then compare their performance indicators with internal or external benchmarking figures. Benchmark data can be obtained through several reputable organizations, including Practice Support Resources, Inc. and Medical Group Management Association.

The following are factors to measure regularly:

- Gross collection ratio
- Net collection ratio
- Days in A/R (accounts receivable)
- Adjustment ratio

More involved analysis might involve the billings per patient or the revenue per patient, expenses per patient, and salary rate per patient. Such performance indicators are highlighted in Figure 13-4.

IMPROVING PERFORMANCE

Most practices can improve performance of their billing and revenue cycle by addressing the following five key areas:

1. **Training.**   All staff members involved in the revenue cycle process should be provided training regarding the fundamentals of creating a bill, how to submit the claims and bill the patient, and how to get the bill paid. Where once the billing process was focused in the billing office itself, the entire office staff is now responsible for getting the medical bill paid. The staff should be educated in the requirements of the different managed care plans with which the practice has agreements, the importance of collecting co-payments at the time of the visit, and awareness of fraud procedures, which the practice furnishes, that will be subject to denial or rejection. The ongoing training for billing and coding personnel regarding regulatory and coding changes should be furnished at least on an annual basis.

2. **Staffing Levels.**   Billing and collections departments are often understaffed simply because this is an area that is not in full

FIGURE 13-4

Examples of Performance Indicators

Gross Collection Ratio:
$$\frac{\text{Total Collections Fee for Service}}{\text{Total Gross Charges (billings)}}$$

Net Collection Ratio:
$$\frac{\text{Total Payments (collections)}}{\text{Total Net Charges (charges minus adjustments)}}$$

Accounts Receivable Ratio:
$$\frac{\text{Total Accounts Receivable}}{\text{Average Monthly Adjusted Charges}}$$

Days in A/R: Length in A/R × 30.4

view of managers and physicians. The urgency of adequate staffing is not readily apparent. Physicians will probably notice when nursing staff or front desk staff are short because they process the patients, but when billing functions are left unattended, it may be months before anyone notices it. Staffing levels should be compared to industry benchmarks to verify that there are adequate staff members in place to perform the charge posting, payment posting, and follow-up tasks that need to be done.

3. **Assessing the Information Flow.**   Without charges, nothing can be billed. The practice should periodically follow the service through the charge-capturing process to determine that there are not opportunities for lost revenue, especially if the physicians practice at various satellite locations, hospitals, or nursing homes or provide home health services. Checks and balances can be implemented within the practice to ensure that all of the services rendered are captured and accounted.

4. **Claims Admission.**   Practices that electronically submit claims usually experience a faster turnaround time than those who file on paper, even with paying charges per claim for a clearinghouse. Practices should negotiate with clearinghouses to determine where the best rate for claims submission can be obtained. Overall, electronic filing of claims is less costly and provides a quicker payment turnaround period.

5. **Assessing Charges and Payment Levels.**   An experienced person should oversee the receipts to ensure that the negotiated rate is being paid by managed care plans and that all services that should be paid are being paid. Inappropriate write-offs can be masqueraded as contracted adjustments when, in fact, appeals or further clarification of the claim can be resolved, resulting in the practice receiving its due payment.

    Common types of underpayments fall into one of five categories:

- Underfunding due to late payments
- Fee-schedule changes that are contractually disallowed
- Miscalculation of performance-based bonuses and errors in risk-payment reconciliation
- Inappropriate denials or down-coding of claims
- Nonpayment

The critical element of success in payment recovery is the discovery and documentation of evidence to support underpayment claims and payer contract noncompliance through auditing.

SELF-PAY FOLLOW-UP

It is essential that practices develop a consistent method for follow-up of patient accounts. These outstanding balances can be the responsibility of patients with no insurance or patients who must pay a portion of the bill after their insurance has covered its part. Once the patient receives the bill, it should be paid within 30 days,

TABLE 13-2

Example of a Collection Time Line

Collection Time Line	
30 days	Bill patient
45 days	Call patient regarding bill
60 days	Letter 1
75 days	Letter 2 and call
80 days	Letter 3
90 days	Turn over to collections

unless the patient makes other arrangements. Table 13-2 shows an example of a collection time line.

Telephone calls to patients often result in questions regarding insurance filing, what the insurance carrier allowed, and if secondary insurance was filed. Therefore, it is advisable to have all the information readily available when making the call. Figure 13-5 will assist the caller in assembling information. Figures 13-6, 13-7, and 13-8 show examples of letters that can also assist in the practice's collection process.

SUMMARY

All practice management questions rely on the success of the revenue cycle, from "how much you are able to pay a new employee" to "can we afford a new copy machine." All members of the practice team must realize the importance of successful revenue capture. It is also important for all to realize that the practice does not render medical care in order to make money. The practice collects money in order to be able to render medical care.

All staff members need to recognize their role in the process and make every effort to capture complete insurance information, capture all legitimate billable charges, file claims in an accurate and timely manner, and persistently follow-up on accounts.

RESOURCES

Guidelines for Monitoring a Profitable Practice. Available at: www.practicesupport.com/pubs/gmppsample.html. Accessed on November 9, 2001.

Hayny T. Receivables Management: An Internal Review. Available at: www.mpmnetwork.com/article, Nov/Dec 1999, Vol. 15, No. 3.

Teems C. *Assessing and Improving: Billing and Collections.* Chicago, Ill: American Medical Association Press, 2001.

Welter T, Stevenson P. Calculating Five Types of Typical Underpayments. *Healthcare Financial Management.* October 2001; 55.

F I G U R E 13-5

Example of a Collection Precall Worksheet

COLLECTION PRECALL PLANNING	
Patient's Name	Account/File Number
Address	Home Telephone #
City, State, Zip	Work Telephone #
Responsible Party (if not same)	Telephone (if not same)

General Information:

Dates of Visits	0 – 30	30 – 60	60 – 90	90+	Total

Payments Received:

Dates	Amounts	Source
TOTALS:		

Past Payment Commitments:

Dates	Payment Commitment	Spoke To

New Payment Commitments:

Dates	Payment Commitment	Spoke To

Calls Made By: File Recall Date:

FIGURE 13-6

Example of a First Collection Letter

Date: _____

Patient: _____

Acct. #: _____

Balance Due: $ _____

Dear _____ ;

Your insurance company has paid its portion of your bill. You are now responsible for the remaining balance. Full payment is due, or you must contact this office within 10 days to make suitable payment arrangements. As an added payment option, you may pay by credit card, using the payment form below.

Sincerely,

Physician/Employee Signature
Physician/Employer Name

- -

Amount: $ _____

_____ VISA   _____ MasterCard   _____ American Express   _____ Discover

Card Number: _____

Authorized Signature: _____   Exp. Date: _____

                        (required)   (required)

Printed name: _____   Acct. #: _____

FIGURE 13-7

Example of a Final Collection Letter

Date: _____

Patient: _____

Acct. #: _____

Balance Due: $ _____

Dear _____;

Your account is seriously past due and has been placed with our in-house collection department. Immediate payment is needed to keep an unfavorable credit rating from being reported on this account. If you are unable to pay in full, please call to make acceptable arrangements for payment. Failure to respond to this notice within 10 days will precipitate further collection actions.

Sincerely,

Physician/Employee Signature
Physician/Employer Name

FIGURE 13-8

Balance after Insurance Payment Letter

Date: _____

Patient: _____

Acct. #: _____

Dear _____ ;

A claim was filed for you from our office for services rendered on _____. Your insurance carrier has responded, and the following amount is your portion to pay:

$ _____ .

Please mail your check today or complete the easy credit card payment option form below and return it in the enclosed envelope.

If you have any questions or need to arrange a payment plan, please feel free to call.

Sincerely,

Physician/Employee Signature
Physician/Employer Name

- -

Amount: $ _____

_____ VISA   _____ MasterCard   _____ American Express   _____ Discover

Card Number: _____

Authorized Signature: _____   Exp. Date: _____

Printed name: _____   Acct. #: _____
              (required)   (required)

chapter 14

Improving Performance Using Benchmarks

Benchmarking is the continuous process of measuring productivity, costs, and quality using standard measures and comparing them against those of others in the industry. Medical practices conduct this process to identify areas that need improvement or to help them determine the reasons why certain aspects of the practice are not working as expected. Even if the practice is doing well, it is advisable to undergo the benchmarking process at least annually to help identify trends, show the practice where they are in comparison to others in the field, and help identify areas that might lead to problems if not corrected. Benchmarking can also be the impetus for change.

Medical practices, as with other businesses, must focus on keeping their revenues high and their expenses low. Benchmarking will help in this process.

Questions that benchmarking can help answer include:

■ Are the physicians' incomes reasonable given their productivity?
■ Is the billing office doing an adequate job of collecting?
■ Are excessive overhead or operating problems caused by inappropriate staffing levels?
■ Are utilization patterns reasonable?

BENCHMARKING PROCESS

To begin the benchmarking process, the practice must have a clear vision of what it hopes to accomplish. Are practice expenses too high? Is patient satisfaction an issue? Does the practice have the right amount of staff? Write in one sentence what the practice hopes to gain from the undertaking. This will help the practice stay on track throughout the comparison process.

Next, determine what is to be compared. Most practices will want to monitor four key areas:

■ Provider productivity
■ Charge per visit indicators
■ Accounts receivables performance
■ Expenses

Additional benchmarks may be monitored as they pertain to quality of care, outcomes, and patient satisfaction. As with any new endeavor, keep the benchmarking process manageable. By comparing a few key indicators the first year and successfully implementing changes, the practice can then broaden its scope in subsequent exercises.

Next, form the team. Decide who is going to be responsible for the process. At this stage, it is important to have leadership involvement and support for the success of the project. However, it is also important to have staff member buy-in. The more people in the organization who believe in the project, the more successful it will be.

To begin the process, obtain viable benchmarks from one of the health care resources available on the market, including (but not limited to):

Practice Support Resources, Inc
4230 Phelps Road, Suite E
Independence, MO 64055
(816) 478-8766
www.practicesupport.com

Cost Survey (annual publication)
Medical Group Management Association
104 Inverness Terrace East
Englewood, CO 80112
(877) 275-6462 (toll-free)
www.mgma.com

Healthcare Benchmarks Newsletter of Best Practices
(monthly publication)
American Health Consultants
3525 Piedmont Road NE
Building 6, #400
Atlanta, GA 30305
(404) 262-7436
www.ahcpub.com

The practice can access standards for accounts receivable collection, physician productivity, practice capacity, staffing FTEs, and salary, profitability, and operating cost. Used correctly, benchmarking standards can provide a standard for comparison as long as the practice takes into consideration the variances of individual practices. It may be preferable to use two sources for comparison, although it is not necessary.

In selecting benchmarks, take precautions to ensure that similar practices are being compared. For example, typically productivity levels differ between hospital-owned practices and private practices. There will also be a difference in the staffing requirements depending on what is performed in-house by the practice and what is provided by a hospital, MSO, or performed by an outside source. Other factors affecting the comparison will include patient socioeconomic demographics, managed care infiltration, office automation, and physician practice styles.

To begin the process, gather as much information about your practice's performance for the past 3-, 6-, or 12-month period depending on how often benchmarks are compared. Information should include:

■ Copies of physician appointment schedules
■ Computer printout of CPT codes, broken down by provider
■ The number of new patients seen in the past year by provider
■ Gross charges by provider
■ Copies of fee schedule(s)
■ Printout of monthly charges, payments, and adjustments
■ Report, broken down by provider
■ Report, broken down by payer
■ Total physician compensation
■ Profit and Loss Statement
■ Total staffing costs
■ Total benefits costs

For example, if a family practice wants to measure provider productivity, it may gather benchmarks as shown in Table 14-1, with the process looking something like the example shown in Table 14-2.

When compiling office information, bear in mind that benchmarking will only be as valuable as the reliability of the data being used. Factors that can affect data reliability are:

■ Physician productivity information
■ Payer mix
■ Ability to track necessary data
■ Existence of appropriate historical data
■ Ancillary production
■ Credit for physician extenders
■ Upcoding
■ Downcoding
■ Billing and collections
■ Payer mix
■ Account write-off policies
■ Policies for recognizing capitated charges
■ Staffing levels
■ Specialty mix

TABLE 14-1

Productivity Benchmarks

Productivity Measure	Benchmarks	Practice
Ambulatory Encounters	4,400	
Surgical/Anesthesia Cases	230	
RVUs	5,000	
Gross Professional Charges	$300,000 (TC/PE Excluded)	
Total Medical Collections	$375,000 (TC/PE Included)	

TABLE 14-2

Productivity Benchmark Process

Measurement	Source 1	Source 2	Practice
Charges/provider			
Visits/provider			
Hours worked/provider			
Number of new patients			
% of visits, new			
Physician compensation			
% of physician compensation to gross charges			
Total operating exp.			
Average charge/visit			
Average revenue/visit			
Average cost/visit			
Distribution by code, new patient visits			
# of major procedure 1			
# of major procedure 2			
# of major procedure 3			
Fee schedule comparison			
Gross collection percentage			
Net collection percentage			
Days in A/R			
A/R percentage by aging			
Staff FTE per provider			
Staff payroll + benefits as percent of revenue			
Provider compensation as percent of revenue			
Other expenses by category			
Operating overhead			

- Clinic size
- Definitions used for position descriptions
- Physician productivity
- Payer-delegated functions
- Expenses
- Geographic variances in cost
- Specialty mix
- Categorizing expenses

Once the benchmarking process has been completed, take steps to make improvements. Many benchmarking efforts end up collecting dust on a shelf. The most critical element is to get the involvement of the practice's leaders and physicians in the benchmarking effort. By building agreement early on that the benchmarking process will be used to establish vision, set goals, identify areas for change, and help the practice implement change, the benchmarking process will have a greater opportunity to succeed.

To meet these demands, make a formal presentation of the findings. Keep the presentation simple and straightforward to retain interest. A report that states the original mission of the project, areas compared, and results will be enough information for most people. End the report with conclusions and recommendations for improvement. Give physicians and staff members an opportunity to discuss the findings and recommendations.

Questions for discussion might include:

■ What do we do that is a waste of time, or could be done more efficiently by someone else?

■ If I were spending my own money to pay for this function, what would I change?

■ What machines or technology are available that would do the job better, faster, or cheaper than what we are doing?

In many cases, the benchmarking process and/or the implementation process will require the assistance of an outside facilitator. So, before beginning the process, ask:

■ Do I have the expertise to do this?

■ Do I have the time to do this?

■ Do I need an objective opinion?

Table 14-3 is a handy tool for helping a practice make the most of the benchmarking exercise.

TABLE 14-3

Findings, Causes, and Corrective Action

Findings Causes		Corrective Action	
Productivity			
Overall productivity low	No incentives	Review compensation plan Productivity-based compensation model	
	Small patient base	Benchmark active patients Marketing plan Patient satisfaction survey	
	Poor appt. scheduling	Assess allotted times Staff education Improve efficiencies Inefficient office layout	
Charge per visit low	Low fee schedule	Review fee schedule	
	Poor coding	Physician education	
Collections			
Gross collections low	Poor managed care contracts	Review, renegotiate contracts	
	Fee schedule high	Review fee schedule	
	Denials, rejections	Log denials, rejections	
	Understaffing	Compare staffing ratio	

(continued on next page)

TABLE   14-3

Findings, Causes, and Corrective Action—*continued*

Findings Causes		Corrective Action	
Collections—cont'd			
Net collections low	Poor follow-up on self-pay	Establish policies for collection Establish performance measures	
Acct. over 90 days high	Old accounts not addressed	Develop firm policies	
	Understaffed	Review staffing	
Expenses			
High overhead percentage	High expenses	Review line items	
	Poor revenue	Review productivity Review collections	
Expense per physician high	High salaries	Compare salaries to gross charges	
	Low revenue	Review collections	
Staffing salaries high	High salaries	Compare for area Review turnover rate	
	Overstaffed	Review staffing ratio	
	Revenues low	Review productivity Review collections	
Occupancy expense high	Price per sq. foot high	Consider changing locations	
	Too much space	Sublease space Reduce sq. footage Add ancillary services	
Medical supplies high	Paying high prices	Comparison shop Join buyers group	
	Overstocked/poor inventory control	Safeguard supplies Use purchase orders Just-in-time inventory	
	Overutilization/waste	Identify waste areas Tie to incentive bonus	
	Not capturing charge	Education on injections/supply trays	
Business supplies high	Prices high	Comparison shop Join buyers group	
	Waste	Inventory control Tie to incentive bonus	
	Overstocked	Purchase order system Inventory control	
	Overutilization	Education	

COMMON MISTAKES IN BENCHMARKING[1]

One of the most common mistakes in benchmarking is having an unfocused initiative. By beginning the benchmarking process without a clear picture of its outcome, the process will be jeopardized. The clearer the vision — the more successful the attempts to bring about change.

If benchmark results do not show a compelling need for change, it is unlikely that the initiative will be able to gather enthusiasm for change. If the efforts are seen as being staff driven rather than leader driven, it will not be successful.

The biggest mistake that is made in benchmarking is the "ready, fire, aim" approach. Responding to requests for solutions without really clarifying the problem will doom the change efforts. This goes along with the "quick fix" solution. Keep in mind that if the problem were easy to fix, someone in the practice would have already fixed it. Therefore, look carefully at what appears to be a simple solution— it may not be a helpful solution.

Look at the big picture rather than try to fix each element or isolate an element. Understand the process. Map out workflows. Interview staff members. The greater the understanding of the matter, the greater the chances for success. Involve staff members. The longer lasting changes come from within. The more people that participate in the change process, the greater the buy-in and the greater the chances for sustained success.

Begin the benchmarking process when there is time to devote to it. If the practice is in the process of hiring a new physician, implementing a compliance plan, opening a satellite office, or converting to a new computer system, the benchmarking process will not work. If the benchmarking initiatives compete with other resources for attention, every area will suffer.

SUMMARY

Practices can significantly improve their performance by assessing where they stand in key indicators and comparing their own performance to that of better performing practices. Once this measurement has been conducted, the practice can set definitive steps toward improvement of practice performance.

ENDNOTES

1.   Is your benchmarking missing the mark? *Healthcare Benchmarks Newsletter.* June 1999.

Marketing the Practice

Marketing can increase income, introduce new providers, and improve the practice's image, but for many practices, marketing is simply a matter of putting an advertisement in the local newspaper, redecorating the waiting room, or conducting a patient satisfaction survey. Physicians are often disappointed in the results of these marketing efforts or worse, have no idea if the effort brought any results at all. Patient satisfaction surveys often sit on a shelf as untapped information, efforts at improving customer service show little change, and physicians resort to joining every provider panel in an effort to expand their patient base.

It does not have to be that way. Patient satisfaction surveys can be used to identify problems within the practice that are relatively easy to correct. Staff members who are included in the marketing strategy will work on their own to improve patient satisfaction, and there are many opportunities to build the patient base. To make the time, effort, and expense of marketing worthwhile, a practice should develop a marketing strategy before beginning the process. Developing a marketing plan will help the practice get the most out of its marketing dollar.

DEVELOPING A MARKETING PLAN

To begin developing a plan, set marketing goals. A clearly defined vision of where the practice wants to be in 6 months, 1 year, or 5 years from now will assist in reaching that vision. As in setting all goals, marketing goals should be specific and have a time frame. For example, the practice may want to increase the number of new patients by 5% within the next 6 months. Or the practice may want to raise patient satisfaction by 15% within the same time frame. Some goals may be longer range. For example, the practice may want to grow by 25% within 18 months or open a new diagnostic center within 2 years.

Clearly define the immediate, intermediate, and long-range goals for the practice. Top leaders and managers should work together to develop the marketing plan, and staff members should be involved. Include a representative from each segment of the practice, such as a front desk staff member, someone from the clinical staff, and a representative from the billing office. Not only will they be able to help determine if a plan will or will not work, they will also be able to spread enthusiasm for the plan to their fellow staff members. Depending on the breadth and scope of the vision, the practice may want to involve outside resources to determine the feasibility of the endeavor. Marketing analyses, compliance issues, and project funding may need to involve a team of experts in the field.

Marketing Budget

The first step in developing a marketing plan is to determine a budget with which to fund the project. This can be a number that the practice is comfortable with or a percentage of gross income. There is no set amount for marketing budgets, although 3% to 5% of gross revenues is often used.[1]

Marketing Strategy

As with any plan for self-improvement, a marketing strategy must begin with a self-evaluation. Determine the practice's strengths and weaknesses. What do patients say they like about the practice? What do they complain about? Do they have trouble getting an appointment when they want one or is it impossible to reach the office by telephone? What are the practice's internal strengths and weaknesses? Are the staff a close-knit group that works well together, or does the practice experience physician dissatisfaction and staff turnover?

When finished with this self-analysis, begin looking at the patient base. Where do the practice's patients come from? What is their age, sex, ethnic origin, type of insurance, and chief medical complaints? To determine the answer to these questions, run reports from the practice management system. It may be surprising to learn that what was thought to be the most often treated ailments are, in actuality, not.

Next, look at the referral base. Where do patients come from? If the practice's patients can be tracked by referring physician, this will be an easy task. However, if the practice management system does not track this, then it is beneficial to have the appointment schedulers log in the referring physician's name if you are a specialist. Primary care physicians should also track referrals. It may be surprising to find that many patients select the practice's name out of the provider directory manual because of a referral from another patient. Depending on the studies one believes, physicians still control 70% to 80% of where patients go for outpatient procedures, what hospitals they are admitted to, and what specialists they see.[2]

To assess the competition, begin by listing the top competitors or calling the state medical society or local hospital for a listing of other physicians in a specific specialty in the area. Look at their advertising strategies, with whom they are aligned, and what patients say about them. How are the competitors viewed within the community, and what marketing activities have they tried?

Once the research has been completed, the practice can then develop the time line to complete the steps.

TAKING ACTION ON MARKETING

Once the goals and marketing budget have been set, the practice is ready to put their plan to work. The practice's goal is to determine how to increase the patient base to the desired level. That entails determining from where patients presently come, increasing those numbers, and identifying new sources of patient referrals.

Try to reach out to new patients through:

- The practice's employees
- Workers compensation carriers
- Insurance plans
- Physicians
- Alternative care providers

For example, if most of the practice's patients are referred by other physicians, determine if there are new physicians in the area who could also refer to the practice. A personal visit (either at the hospital or in their office) may prompt referrals from them. Contact the physicians who have referred decreasing numbers of patients to the practice and determine if there is a problem. Provide referring physicians with special access to the office, such as a special referral line or a contact person.

Marketing activities can also be initiated by designing a new practice logo to be prominently displayed on patient information brochures and other literature. Newsletters, Web sites, and patient surveys are also proven methods to attract new patients.

HEALTH CARE MARKETING TRENDS

Following is a list of current trends in health care marketing:

- **Technology.** Practices are continuing to develop Web sites and offer e-mail access to their patients. This trend will continue as forerunners allow patients to schedule their own appointments or electronically access lab results.

- **Relationship building.** This goes back to basics of developing relationships with referring physicians and community relations programs. Health fairs, screenings, and community magazines are good ways to build relationships and create name recognition. This goes hand-in-hand with *buzz marketing*, which involves enlisting individuals who are trendsetters and who influence the opinions of others. This word-of-mouth marketing is highly effective in targeting ethnic or cultural groups or in communicating with teens and young adults who are especially reliant on peer-to-peer communication.

- **Retail marketing.** Selling health care products directly to consumers is another marketing trend. Plastic surgeons and dermatology practices have long offered skin care products in their practices. Other physicians are finding that selling health care products is an effective way to increase revenues — and increase patient satisfaction. However, mixing retail and medicine is not for every practice.

- **Outcomes and ratings.** The Healthplan Employer Data Information Set (HEDIS), which has been around for some time, is the tool managed care plans use to measure the clinical outcomes of patient treatment. Physicians who are able to track how successfully they manage a disease will be in a better negotiating position with managed care plans, and may even be designated a *top quality* provider.

- **Alternative medicine.** Many patients are turning to alternative medicine for treatment of their illnesses. The more informed the physician is about those treatments and their benefits, the more effectively the patient's questions can be handled. Many patients are willing to pay out-of-pocket for alternative medicine. If the practice can understand why patients are seeking alternative medicine, perhaps it can adapt to meet their needs.

See Figure 15-1 for a sample marketing assessment tool worksheet.

FIGURE 15-1

Marketing Assessment Tool Worksheet

MARKETING ASSESSMENT TOOL WORKSHEET
Practice Assessment:
• List 20 most often provided procedures.   • List 5 highest-fee procedures.   • List top 20 diagnosis codes.   • List top 5 payers.   • List top 10 referral sources.   • What do we do well?
Patient Assessment:
• What is age of our patients?   • What is the percentage of each sex?   • What is the ethnic origin?   • What zip codes do they represent?   • Why do patients choose us?
Where is Our Target Market:
• Referring physicians   • Managed care plans   • Employees   • Workers compensation carriers   • Elderly   • Young families
What is the Best Way to Reach Market:
• Personal visit   • Direct mailing   • Word of mouth   • Special accommodations   • Expanded hours (eg, Saturday, evenings)   • Expanded services (eg, health, wellness, alternative)

SUMMARY

Medical practices continually need to market their services. Marketing can be in the form of improving patient satisfaction, making the community aware of available products and services, and improving the practice's image. Practices can make the most of their marketing dollar by developing a marketing budget and strategic plan.

ENDNOTES

1. Anwar R, Capko J. Steps to a strategic marketing plan. *Family Practice Management*. November/December 2000. Available at: www.aafp.org/fpm/. Accessed on November 17, 2001.

2. Fell D. Physician Marketing: Not Overlooking the Obvious. Available at: healthleaders.com/news/features, October 17, 2001. Accessed on December 3, 2001.

RESOURCES

Anwar R, Capko J. Steps to a strategic marketing plan. *Family Practice Management*. November/December 2001. Available at: www.aafp.org/fm. Accessed on November 17, 2001.

Fell D. Physicians Marketing: Not Overlooking the Obvious. Available at: www.healthleaders.com/news/features, October 17, 2001. Accessed on December 3, 2001.

Scott J. The Buzz on 'Buzz Marketing' for Healthcare. Available at: www.healthleaders.com/news/features, Accessed on November 28, 2001.